HOW TO HELP
YOUR CHILD THROUGH SCHOOL

How to help your child through school

Maureen O'Connor

HARRAP
London

First published in Great Britain 1990
by Harrap Books Ltd
Chelsea House, 26 Market Square, Bromley, Kent BR1 3484

© Maureen O'Connor 1990

ISBN 0 245 60027–2

Designed by Paperweight
Printed and bound in Great Britain by
The Guernsey Press, Guernsey, CI

CONTENTS

ACKNOWLEDGEMENTS

The publishers are grateful to HMSO for allowing them to reproduce extracts from *Better Schools*, various Education Acts, *Mathematics in the National Curriculum* and *English in the National Curriculum*. These extracts are reproduced with the permission of the Controller of HMSO.

The extracts from *School is Not Compulsory* on pages 124 and 131, are reproduced by kind permission of Education Otherwise.

The front cover photograph is by J. King (Image House). The back cover photograph is by Robin Anderson.

I

PRE-SCHOOL CHILDREN

The period between birth and the age of five, as every parent knows, is one of remarkable growth. The helpless baby turns with uncanny speed into the lively, running, chattering, demanding five-year-old who is already mentally half-way to adulthood.

We all have the evidence of our own eyes to see that young children learn incredibly quickly in their first five years, with an enthusiasm and an insatiable curiosity which can be a real joy, though sometimes exhausting for everyone else around. What is not nearly so clear-cut is how they learn, and how we can help them to make the maximum progress.

THE EXPERTS' VIEW

For a long time child psychologists accepted the wisdom of a Swiss pioneer in the study of child development, Jean Piaget (1896-1980), who argued from experimental evidence that young children did not gain the ability to think in abstract logical terms much before the age of seven. That view has not been completely discredited, but it has certainly been challenged by researchers who have shown that much younger children can understand and complete some of the tasks Paiget set, so long as they are explained in language that they can understand.

According to Margaret Donaldson, author of an influential book, *Children's Minds*, normal children show a remarkable ability to think and use language before school age as long as, and this is the important point, new words are introduced in 'real life' contexts that they understand. ('Real life' can include stories and films or even the child's own imaginative fantasies as well as the world of family, home and friends in which they live.) This is not really so strange. It is, after all, the way children have used thought and language ever since they first attached names to people and objects in their very first efforts to learn to talk. Mummy and Daddy, a bigger brother, and all the objects around the house, come first; the ability to define and talk about abstract ideas like love and affection, however real they may be, much later.

In fact adults function in exactly the same way for large periods of time. Argument and reasoning divorced from real activities are not the norm for most of the time even in adult life, although they are essential tools if we are to progress intellectually beyond the simplest stage of human development and function adequately in a complex modern society. But for young children, the here and now appears to be the main context in which they learn before the age of five.

LEARNING BY DOING

It follows that children learn a great deal from doing things. And if they are to learn at home – and clearly most of the learning children do between birth and five is going to occur at home – they must be offered the maximum chance to talk, to ask questions and to participate in a wide variety of activities.

Professor Barbara Tizard who with Martin Hughes undertook a survey of young children talking and thinking at home and at school, concluded that the home is a very powerful learning environment and in some respects is far more effective than nursery schooling. The learning they observed covered a wide range of topics – in some homes, plays, games, stories and even formal 'lessons' provided general knowledge and the basis for numeracy and literacy. But the most usual and most effective learning occurred simply during the wide range of activities which go on at home anyway.

Simply being around with Mother – or another adult – talking, arguing and endlessly asking questions, provides children with extensive opportunities to learn. Close observation by Tizard showed children talking and learning while they helped to plan, cook and clear away meals, wash and iron, look after younger brothers and sisters, pets, and gardens, or listened to discussions about money, wages and bills, visited relatives or had visitors at home. In addition they learned about the wider world by seeing parents and others going to and from work, watching older children go to school and bring work home, and by visiting neighbourhood shops, schools, clinics, libraries, markets, garages, parks, and swimming-pools, going to the zoo and going on holiday, by bus or train, car or plane.

All these activities provide the child with a wide range of subjects and events to discuss, people to meet, and places to visit. They also provide a range of social relationships and the sight of a variety of people involved in different roles and activities.

FINDING OUT HOW THE WORLD WORKS
The second aspect of learning at home which Barbara Tizard discovered was important – and which could not easily take place at school – was the sense in which the child and its family shared a past and a future which interwove naturally into discussions and events. Teachers cannot easily say to a child 'Do you remember?', or promise that at some future time something interest-ing or exciting will happen. Family members can and do, placing the child in a context of relationships and a time-scale which enhances what a child understands about the world and how it makes sense.

It is difficult to imagine being three or four and

understanding as little about how the world works as a child of that age does. In a situation where so little is known, nothing can actually be ruled out unless there are powerful reasons for doing so. If you do not know that the world turns on its axis, pretty well anything at all could make the sun rise in the morning and set at night. If you do not understand that people work away from home at specific jobs, Daddy's or Mummy's departure in the morning and return at night could be for any number of almost magical reasons. The possibilities are so unlimited that it is easy to see why children can learn only from their own very concrete experiences at first. They appear to have to move in stages to anything larger.

HELPING CHILDREN LEARN AT HOME

So what do children need to help them learn at home, and make the most of the exciting years before school when so much progress can be made, and so much groundwork laid for success later?

The first thing all the experts say is that learning at this age should not be a chore – most of it will occur naturally without any noticeable effort anyway. But whether learning is unpremeditated or planned, it should above all be fun. Children of this pre-school age who are pushed in a direction in which they do not want to go will be bored, will switch off and will learn nothing.

The first essential is that the person who is at home with the pre-school child – often the mother but not always – should recognize the importance of talk, and find time to listen to the child, answer endless questions and ask a few well-chosen ones in return. One observation that Barbara Tizard made in nursery schools is that teachers, in the more limited time they have available to talk to pupils, often start conversations by asking questions, and that children are often curiously unforthcoming in reply. In the more relaxed and natural situation of the home, it is usually the child who asks questions during a conversation, asking for the simple reason that a reply of some sort, and probably an explanation, is needed.

We have all become exasperated by two-year-olds at the 'Why?' stage: 'Why are we going out? Why do we have to go to the shops? Why do I have to put my gloves on? Why must I go in the buggy? Why can't I walk?' Most parents in the end resort to the old stand-by 'Because I say so'. But those why's , and the what's and how's and what if's which follow over the next couple of years are a sign of a mind trying to make sense of an immensely complicated world, often without the vocabulary which makes it easy enough for an adult to understand.

So patience is called for, and some appreciation of how a child is searching for new words all the time to help understand the world. So if the first rule for the under fives is talk, talk, talk, the second is never talk down. Moo-cows and baa-lambs and puffer-trains are not going to help much in the real world of communication into which the five-year-old has to be launched so very quickly. Pet names in the family are one thing – and may survive into adult life. My family laughed about the character my small son called 'Porence' in the *Magic Roundabout* television cartoon for years. But comic baby names for real things are going to be a disadvantage at school.

So use the real words. Pronunciation difficulties will sort themselves out in time as the child becomes more fluent and confident with the more difficult sounds of the English language like R and L and TH. By the age of five most children will have mastered the pronunciation of English sufficiently well to make themselves understood to strangers outside the immediate family. That is going to be vital when school starts. But they only learn by constant practice and by hearing words correctly and clearly pronounced for them. Don't make a chore out of correcting a child's pronunciation. Some children are slower than others to develop the control needed for certain speech sounds. It should come right in time. But if speech does appear to be a problem at around four – and especially if outsiders are having difficulty in understanding what a child is saying – then it is not too early to seek advice. A doctor might recommend the help of a speech therapist who will spend some time with the child, and offer advice on what can be done to improve the child's speech at home. The aim should certainly be to have a child speaking clearly enough to be easily understood by the time full-time school starts at five.

The third rule has to be: always try to find some answer to a child's questions. It is often easier to brush them off with a brusque 'I don't know' or 'Ask me later' or even, under stress, 'Do shut up'. But it is a temptation to be resisted. Children need to ask questions, they need answers, and if possible they need an adult with the time to think about just why the question has been asked in the first place, and to make sure that the answer provided is as full and informative as possible, and that any new words which have to be used are very carefully explained. And if you listen carefully, you will realize that the questions are sometimes not even put directly. Take this comment, out of doors on a summer day, which starts with quite a sophisticated comparison for a child under five:

'Mum, that plane sounds like a motor-bike.'

The child's mother might answer, simply 'Yes', almost without a thought. But given a moment's consideration, she might prefer to say:

'Yes, that's because it's not a jet. It's a propeller plane. Look at the front of it.'

And you can imagine the questions which will follow: 'What is a jet? What is a propeller?', and so on until most parents might well run out of answers. And then what if you genuinely don't know? There is no shame in admitting it, of course, but a lot of good education will follow if you not only admit it but suggest that there are ways of finding out, by looking in a book, for instance, or taking a trip to the library. And if you think that books for the under fives do not explain how aeroplanes work – in very simple terms, of course – then you have not been in touch with factual books for young children lately.

It is a two-way process, of course. There is nothing wrong with asking children questions designed to make them think as well as following up their own spontaneous interests. But don't make them too abstract. Make use of the things that are going on around you both at home or in the neighbourhood. 'Why is this a good day to dry the sheets out of doors?' for instance. Or 'Why are those men digging a hole in the road, do you think?' A whole world of everyday events that adults take for granted are unknown, mysterious and potentially fascinating to a child under five.

Again, it is not necessary to make a chore out of developing children's vocabulary, but there are lots of games that can be played to extend their knowledge of colours, sounds, animals, relationships – who is an aunt and who is a cousin? – spatial words like in, on, under, over, above, and so on, transport, or anything else which particularly interests the child. Long words don't frighten small children if they understand them and have a genuine curiosity about them. Think of all the five or six-year-olds who can tell you the difference between Brontosaurus and Tyrannosaurus Rex.

It is not only conversation which helps children's learning either. There is plenty of evidence that children's later ability to learn to read and write fluently depends to a large extent on their familiarity with books, stories, and even nursery rhymes. Books can be obtained fairly easily these days from supermarkets as well as traditional bookshops, and they can be borrowed even more cheaply from the children's library. And many children are happy to browse through the colour magazines, and even catalogues, and learn new words that way.

The old nursery rhymes and songs are fun, of course, although to some extent they have been allowed to drop out of fashion. That is a pity because there is evidence that their rhythms and rhymes can help to develop children's discrimination between sounds: Jill, hill, down, crown, after, laughter, wall, fall, men, again, and so on. This will be invaluable when a child begins to learn to read and has to distinguish between the different sounds which go to make up words. So it's a good idea to see how many you can remember or to buy or borrow a good illustrated collection. Some have survived for hundreds of years, and have not lost their freshness yet.

Most children also have toys, and almost any toy can be 'educational'. Putting a doll to bed, building a motorway for toy cars, or riding a tricycle, all extend children's imagination and co-ordination and should not be despised. But of the so-called 'educational toys' some are perhaps more valuable than others, and they need not be expensive. Building bricks and construction toys are essential for all children, girls as well as boys. It is argued these days that girls' poorer performance at certain spatial aspects of mathematics in later school life is largely because of the fact that they are often denied Lego and similar building toys with which their brothers play – and learn – from the age of three or four. On the other hand, there is no reason why boys should not gain a lot from playing with toys regarded as traditionally female, like dolls, as it is from that sort of experience that they will learn about and act out family roles. After all, fathers very often bath the baby and change a nappy these days, so there is no need for little boys, or more likely their fathers, to feel embarrassed by that sort of play.

Don't buy toys on impulse. They can be very expensive and may lose their appeal very quickly if they do not have some durable attraction. And both safety and suitability for the age group have to be carefully considered too. Staff in the more 'educational' toy shops will often advise on what is the 'best buy' for the age group.

Books and toys are discussed in more detail in Chapter 16.

Children also need access to creative materials like paints and crayons, something to model with – dough is just as good as expensive Plasticine, and can be coloured with non-toxic food colourings – and bits and pieces to make models or dressing-up outfits with. Children learn an enormous amount from reproducing their world, and imaginary worlds, in games.

None of this is particularly expensive, and don't forget that children can play and learn just by being around the house, or garden or park, and being allowed to experiment with things: saucepans make a wonderful band, if you can stand the racket. Setting the table is a good time to practise counting and matching. Let children help to weigh things in the kitchen, or do a bit of measuring with the extending ruler if there is decorating going on.

There is a lot of worry expressed in high places about the effect of television on young children, but television can be educational as well as mindless or frightening, and can be used with discrimination. Some British children's television programmes are amongst the best in the world, and are aimed specifically at the under fives. Ideally an adult should watch television with a young child, so that someone is available to follow up what is going on on the screen and answer questions. It should be an opportunity for adult and child to share an experience, and it will be far more educational that way than if the child is dumped in front of the set to give a parent a quiet half-hour: though the latter can be important for family harmony, too!

SHOULD YOU TEACH YOUR CHILD TO READ?

There are several pre-school reading and writing schemes on the market to tempt parents to spend a lot of money on pre-school 'education', and everyone has heard of four-year-olds who are fluent readers. There is some evidence that children who have learnt the shapes and sounds and names of letters at least before they start school will get off to a flying start.

But there are several points to keep in mind. If you are going to spend money on reading-books or 'schemes' it is worth getting professional advice about their quality from an expert locally. Your playgroup supervisor, nursery-class teacher or primary school head should be happy to offer advice. Then remember that children's 'readiness' to begin to read develops from all the other pre-school activities described here, and in particular depends upon their spoken vocabulary. A typical five-year-old has a vocabulary of about 2,000 words and most teachers reckon this is the minimum needed to start reading. As far as writing is concerned, children's ability to co-ordinate eye and hand develops at different rates in different children, and the ability to write depends very much on that motor co-ordination. Some children may have it before five, others will not, and will find attempts to learn to write very frustrating. The last thing parents should do is make pre-school children feel like failures because they have not been able to meet parental expectations.

Teachers, of course, used to say that parents should NEVER teach their children to read or write at home.

That view has been very much modified recently, and most primary teachers now accept that some children are ready, and will enjoy, some reading and writing work before the age of five. But the emphasis should be on enjoyment and on a short period of teaching each day to supplement the daily story and other activities at home or in the nursery school. The approach to reading can start with simple word recognition: the child's name, or the word 'dog' or 'mum' written on the bottom of a picture. The number of words recognized will soon expand, and the child can be encouraged to point them out in story-books, or to make labels for common items around the house – even Mum and Dad if they can bear it.

Letters should be taught by their sounds (a for apple, b for button, k for cat) and by the alphabetic names, ABC. Writing should begin with simple copying of familiar words. Children who are keen and interested and find the whole process fun will set their own pace. But it should never be a chore: children should never be shouted at or even made to feel uncomfortable if they fail, and never pressed to continue if they become bored.

PRE-SCHOOL SCHEMES

There are an increasing number of pre-school 'packs' and 'schemes' on the market which aim to help parents of young children to do all the 'right' things at home to help educational progress later. They vary from completely 'over-the-top' schemes which purport to teach tiny toddlers to recognize words on flash-cards (at a time when most toddlers have far more important things to learn like an adequate spoken vocabulary), to better researched and more useful schemes which offer parents books, tapes, and ideas for activities which they might not think of or be able to provide for themselves.

Most experts, however, suggest that before a family

takes on an expensive commitment to buy regular instalments of a pre-school scheme, they should make sure they are taking advantage of everything else that is available in the home or neighbourhood or pre-school group, very often free. Books, toys, either bought or borrowed from a library, television programmes designed for the pre-school child, and lots of outings and activities, can probably provide just as much. But if a family feels that a pre-school learning scheme might be helpful to a child, it is not a bad idea to take the literature and any sample material along to a local playgroup organizer or nursery teacher to ask for a professional opinion.

MOTHER-AND-TODDLER GROUPS

Some health clinics and community groups organize special groups for mothers with children under three which enable them to meet and play together, and enable mothers to come into contact with friends with similar family interests and problems. The health visitor should be able to advise where a local mother-and-toddler group is based.

Mothers who take very young children to such groups are often surprised at the children's reluctance to 'make friends' or play together. In fact it is quite normal for one and two-year-olds to prefer playing alongside other children rather than with them. This does not mean that they are not enjoying the experience of being with other children, simply that they are not yet confident enough to make relationships with them. That will come later, as will the ability to share toys and other activities. At first a toddler will play alongside the rest of the group, and will often wish to make sure that Mother – or another familiar adult – is around.

If there is not a mother-and-toddler group locally, then it should be possible to establish one either formally, perhaps at the local clinic, with the advice and assistance of the health visitor, in co-operation with a local playgroup, or with a few like-minded friends at home. Very young children probably do not want to meet other children for more than one or two mornings a week at first, so the organization involved is not heavy.

2

NURSERY EDUCATION

DOES IT MAKE A DIFFERENCE?

Britain has been slow to extend education to children younger than the official school starting age of five. Within Western Europe, Austria, Belgium, Denmark, the Netherlands, Germany, France and Italy, all have a considerably higher proportion of four-year-olds in some sort of nursery education, and even Spain is ahead of us. At the last count, 44 per cent of British three and four-year-olds were in either nursery education or infant school reception classes, and a whole array of campaigners, from the main opposition parties and the trades unions to groups of concerned mothers with young children, were still campaigning, as they have been doing since the mid-1960s, for an expansion of pre-school provision. The most recent call for expansion has come from the Conservative controlled Select Committee on Education, which in January 1989 called on the Government to fulfil Mrs Thatcher's pledge of 1972, when she was Education Minister, to provide nursery education places for all three and four-year-olds whose parents wanted it for them.

But does pre-school education make any long-term difference to children's performance in school? And if it does, what can the individual parent do about it?

Research in the 1960s seemed to indicate that pre-school experience did help children to learn when they moved on to formal school at five – or in other countries, at six or seven. There appeared to be measurable intellectual benefits, as well as the social advantages

14

which infants' teachers commonly commented on when they received children with some pre-school experience. Much was made of the possibility that children from disadvantaged backgrounds could be given a headstart – the actual name of one American pre-school programme – if they began their education earlier.

But research during the Seventies produced some disillusion: the intellectual benefits at that stage did not appear to be long-lasting. In fact they seemed to disappear within a few years of transfer to a normal school.

But the longer the research into the long-term performance of children who have had pre-school experience has continued, the more it has tended to confirm the original view that the benefits of nursery education are long-lasting and, over a period of years, – extremely cost-effective for society. Students who had pre-school experience have been found not only to be intellectually ahead two, five and even ten years later, but also to be better adjusted socially, to be less likely to drop out of school early, and less likely to become delinquent. In America, disadvantaged three-year-olds who had two years' experience of the structured High/Scope pre-school programme emerged at the age of nineteen with more qualifications, higher career aspirations and fewer recorded criminal offences than similar children who had had no pre-school experience.

Professor Barbara Tizard, whose research into children at home showed how effective parents were in helping them to learn, emphasized in her book (*Young Children Learning*) that the fact children learn a great deal at home should not be taken as an argument for not providing nursery education. Children's needs are various, and good nursery provision can add to the intellectual development fostered at home, and also provide some experiences and activities which it is hard for homes to offer: contact with other children and adults, the chance to belong to a group, a wider variety of activities and play-equipment, an essential preparation for school.

For the average family with pre-school children, though, the immediate consideration will not be long-term benefit so much as the chance pre-school education gives children to mix with others of their own age, learn the skills of belonging to a group before they have to go to school at five, and the respite pre-school care gives busy parents who may simply need a break from their young children. And with a future Queen (the Princess of Wales) who worked as a nursery assistant and who has very publicly taken her sons to nursery school at the age of three, there is maybe the very understandable feeling that what is good enough for little princes is good enough for us all.

HOW TO FIND A PRE-SCHOOL PLACE

Provision for the under fives is a patchwork, some of it provided by Local Education Authorities, some by Social Services departments, some voluntarily run, and some part of the commercial network of private schools. Here is a brief guide to what is available.

DAY NURSERIES

These are run by Social Services departments for children between the ages of 0 and 5. They are staffed by nurses and nursery nurses, not trained teachers, and provide full and part-time care mainly for families for whom care of young children at home is difficult for some social or medical reason. Some day nurseries are now run in conjunction with nursery schools or classes so that the older children can have the benefit of the attention of trained nursery teachers as well as the care staff during school hours. Day nurseries are few and far between and places extremely difficult to obtain unless there are pressing social reasons to justify one.

NURSERY SCHOOLS

A nursery school is a separate school solely for three to five-year-olds, with its own head-teacher and staff of nursery teachers and nursery nurses. Educationally, it serves the same function as:

NURSERY CLASSES

These are classes for the under fives attached to a primary school and under the control of the primary head-teacher. Both nursery schools and nursery classes are staffed more favourably than infants' classes, with generally between eight and twelve children to each adult, compared to the infant class ratio of fifteen to thirty with one teacher. The more favourable ratio is made possible by the employment of nursery nurses in nursery schools and classes. Nursery nurses have a shorter training and are less well paid than teachers.

PRE-SCHOOL PLAYGROUPS

These are pre-school groups usually run by or in close co-operation with parents. The playgroup movement was started in the 1960s by a group of young mothers frustrated at being unable to find nursery education for their children. What began as a tiny volunteer movement grew over the next two decades into a movement catering for more than 500,000 under fives. Parents may be expected to help in the running of a playgroup as part of the price of having a place for their child. Playgroups are usually held in rented accommodation – church halls, or empty school classrooms – and although they may receive grant aid from the Local Authority they will usually also charge a small sessional fee per child.

Although some playgroups, especially in inner city areas, may be run by charitable groups like the Save the

Children Fund, most are still run on a co-operative basis by parents. Many of the adults involved in the day-to-day organization of playgroups have now received some training, which is frequently available through local further education colleges or under the auspices of the umbrella body, the Pre-School Playgroups Association. Some even employ trained teachers or nursery nurses. Mothers or fathers without training, though, may be expected to offer some regular help to the group. In the view of the PPA, one of the strongest arguments in favour of the retention of playgroups as part of a network of pre-school provision is that the involvement of parents is beneficial both to the children in playgroups and to families as a whole. Even if the money becomes available to expand pre-school services on a more formal basis, the PPA wants the playgroup tradition of parental involvement to survive.

SOME FACTS AND FIGURES ABOUT PLAYGROUPS

In 1987 the Pre-School Playgroups Association had 422 branches catering for 450,000 three to five-year-olds. The majority of groups cater mainly for three and four-years olds, but almost a third also offer mother-and-toddler sessions, and seven per cent include the under threes, usually accompanied by a parent or other carer. About two per cent of groups offer full day care. The average cost of a playgroup place is now £1.01 per child per session, and most playgroups run between three and five sessions a week. Only thirty-two per cent of playgroups receive any help by way of grant from their Local Authority, but the size of grants varies widely: the majority received £200 or less, in Inner London in 1987 the average grant was £4,227.

PRIVATE NURSERY SCHOOLS

The private sector is expanding its services for the under

fives and in general offers similar facilities to those in State nursery schools. The private sector, though, also includes rather more formal schools and classes for the under fives, often attached to prep schools for older children, where the emphasis is likely to be on formal learning of the 3Rs rather than learning through play. Some private nursery schools or kindergartens insist on uniforms for their children and may regard their main function as preparing children for a hierarchy of private prep and secondary schools from the earliest possible age.

The private sector also includes most schools run according to the principles of the Italian educationalist Maria Montessori (1870-1952), who had a clearly worked out philosophy of learning involving experiment and wide experience of different sensory stimuli. Montessori teaching methods are seldom taken much beyond the early primary years in this country, although in some European countries there are also Montessori secondary schools.

FAMILY CENTRES

Some Local Authorities are experimenting with 'family' or 'community' centres which offer a range of services for families with young children under one roof. A typical centre might offer full day care for a small number of children with special needs – single-parent families where the parent is working full-time, or children living in exceptionally poor housing conditions – plus a mother-and-toddler group, and playgroup or nursery facilities. Typically such centres are jointly funded by Social Services and education departments, and some involve parents in the organization and day-to-day running of the centre.

HOW TO FIND OUT WHAT IS AVAILABLE

Day nurseries

The local Social Services department or the health visitor will have information on day-nursery places, which may be reserved for families in particular difficulties.

State nursery schools and classes

The Local Education Authority will provide a list of its pre-school provision. In most areas nursery schools and classes are over-subscribed and there may be a waiting list, or entry may be delayed for a term or two after a child is three. It is possible to apply for a place in a nursery class even if a child is not expected to proceed to the reception class of that particular school. In fact if primary school admissions are operated on a catchment area principle, a Local Authority may not be able to guarantee that all children in a nursery class will be able to proceed to the next stage in that school if some children live some distance away. Priority will be given to children in the immediate area even if they have not attended the nursery class.

Playgroups

The Social Services department keeps a register of playgroups, which have to meet certain criteria on accommodation, etc.

Private pre-school provision

Private nursery schools also have to be registered with the Social Services department. Local Education Authorities also generally keep a list of private schools.

IF THERE IS A CHOICE

Few families who cannot afford private school fees have much choice of pre-school provision, for the simple reason that State nursery schools and classes are very unevenly distributed from one Local Authority to another – you are much more likely to find a place in a city, where nursery education has been expanding over recent years, than in a rural area, where some county councils provide no pre-school places at all. Playgroups have in general been set up to fill the gaps in State provision.

There is little evidence to suggest that one type of provision is more effective than another: a good playgroup may be better than a badly run nursery school. It is the quality of the experience that seems to count.

So if choice is available in a sector which spans very modest voluntary playgroups and well-funded market oriented private kindergartens, then here are some criteria upon which to make a choice:

1. The ratio of adults to children. Ironically the regulations which apply to playgroups provide for a better ratio of adults to children, eight to one, than recommended by the Department of Education and Science for maintained nursery schools and classes, thirteen to one. In the pre-school sector not all the adults involved will be trained but all provision should include some staff with training: either a fully trained nursery teacher, a nursery nurse or an adult with a playgroup leader's qualification.
2. The standard of accommodation and equipment. There should be enough space and equipment to enable children to play active games both indoors and out, and a good supply of books, educational games and toys, and space for 'messy' activities like painting, modelling and sand and water play.
3. An organized structure to the day or half day. Parents and even children often complain that some playgroups are unstructured, noisy and wild. There should be a structure to the sessions which allows time

for active and quiet activities without one interfering with the other. Children should not be allowed to monopolize one type of toy or activity. There should be time and opportunity for children and adults to engage in talk and discussion together, and set times for stories and musical activities.

4. The level to which parents are involved in the children's education. Playgroups have a long tradition of involving parents, particularly, but not exclusively, mothers, in the organization and running of their activities. Many nursery schools have also now realized the value of involving parents in their work and ask for volunteers to help. Even if it is not possible to commit that amount of time to the nursery, it is important that parents should always feel welcome in the group or class, and able to ask advice on any problems. The education of pre-school children occurs at home as well as in a pre-school institution.

5. Are there good links with the next stage of education? Ideally children should 'move up' with their friends from pre-school provision to primary school and this is obviously much easier when the nursery class or playgroup are in the same building as the next school. Where this is not so, some effort should be made by the school or group to make the transition to school as easy as possible, by way of regular contacts with teachers, visits, etc.

HOW TO SET UP A PLAYGROUP

The first three requirements are personnel, premises and good advice. The first can be any group of willing parents, provided that one member is either already qualified as a play-leader, or is willing to train – if a suitable training course is available locally. Most playgroups designate one playleader and have a rota system to provide additional adult help. The PPA suggests that a playgroup should never be run with fewer than two adults present in case of accident or emergency. Premises vary widely – some playgroups are held in church or voluntary group halls, some in empty primary classrooms, with the co-operation of the head-teacher, and some in private houses. The PPA advises that a playgroup should not exceed twenty-four children at any one session, because of the pressure of noise and stress on young children, and many groups are considerably smaller than that. Small groups can be run satisfactorily in a private house.

Good advice is readily available from the PPA, which works on a regional basis and can usually put a potential playgroup in touch with its local organizer. It also provides a wide range of literature for playgroup leaders and other involved adults, and is involved in many of the training schemes run in conjunction with local colleges.

Playgroups in England and Wales must be registered under the Nursery and Childminders Regulation Act 1948. The precise requirements vary from one Local Authority area to another, some interpreting the regulations more sympathetically than others. Groups which are attended by toddlers accompanied by a parent do not need to register as parents or guardians remain responsible for their children while they are in the group.

Adult/child ratio
The PPA recommends a ratio of one adult to every eight children as a maximum, but one to six as more desirable. If children with special educational needs are attending the group, then they advise that extra adult help may be required. The PPA believes that the play-leader, or any adult who is to take charge of the group, should have some training, and that if possible other adults involved should have had some training too. The standard foundation course for play-leaders involves

120 hours of study.

Insurance
Playgroups need to take out insurance for all risks, i.e. public liability, theft, personal accident, etc. The PPA offers a tailor-made scheme. Groups should also take advice on fire precautions on the premises, and make adequate arrangements for first aid, and adult cover in the event of an accident involving a child being taken to hospital.

Records
The PPA advises that a daily attendance record should be kept, together with details of contact numbers for parents or other responsible adults, and the child's doctor, in the case of emergency, and records of illnesses and immunizations.

Toilets etc
The regulations require one toilet for ten children and one washbasin for every six, but some Local Authorities are prepared to be more flexible, and the PPA recommends that two toilets for a playgroup of twenty-four children is adequate.

Health
The Local Authority may require adults to have a chest X-ray, although some will accept proof of a BCG test as sufficient evidence of good health. The PPA is concerned at the risk of Rubella (German measles) infection to pregnant mothers and believes that playgroups should encourage immunization for participating women who have not had the infection to cut down the risk of the spread of the disease. They advise that children with infectious diseases, apart from colds, should be excluded from playgroups, particularly in view of the risk of the spread of infection to younger brothers and sisters.

FOUR-YEAR-OLDS IN PRIMARY SCHOOLS

An increasing number of Local Authorities are admitting
four-year-olds to primary schools although there is no
legal obligation to admit a child – or for a child to attend
– until the beginning of the term after their fifth birthday.
The latest figures from the Department of Education and
Science for 1987 show a remarkable 73 per cent of four-
year-olds in school before their fifth birthday.

There are two main reasons why Local Authorities are
pursuing this policy. Money is short for the expansion of
nursery education and until very recently the number of
children in primary schools has been falling. A simple
answer to the lack of nursery places might appear to
Local Authorities to be to offer four-year-olds reception
class places where the space is available.

They are bolstered in this belief by research that shows
that the traditional method of admitting children to
school as they reach either the term before or the term
after their fifth birthday, has distinct disadvantages for
children born in the summer months. If they do not start
their first year at school until the beginning of the
summer term, or even the autumn term after their
birthday, they will ultimately receive one or two terms
less infants' schooling than children in the same year
group whose birthdays fall earlier in the year. As they
move through the school system, June, July and August
born children will 'move up' from year to year with the
children born up to nine months earlier, and therefore
entitled to start school earlier too. Research shows that
they have great difficulty in ever catching up. Local
Authorities feel that they are therefore justified in
admitting children to school in some cases almost as
soon as they are four to overcome this disadvantage.

SHOULD YOU ACCEPT A SCHOOL PLACE AT FOUR?

The two main national associations concerned with pre-school children, the Pre-School Playgroups Association (PPA) and the British Association for Early Childhood Education (BAECE) are extremely disturbed by the trend towards admitting four-year-olds to school, and said as much in their evidence to the House of Commons Education Select Committee inquiry into educational provision for the under fives in 1988.

They argued that infants' teachers are trained to teach the basic primary school subjects, and that many four-year-olds are not sufficiently mature intellectually for formal school work, nor are they always emotionally capable of coping with a full school day in an institution of 200 or 300 children. Their advice to parents offered a school place for a four-year-old is this:

Remember that there is no legal obligation on a parent to send a four-year-old to school. On the other hand, a school must make a place available in the term after a child's fifth birthday if there is space for that child. An early admissions policy cannot therefore be enforced by law: it is an option for parents to consider.

There is no evidence that an earlier start in school enables 'summer born' children to catch up on the children in the same year group: they will always be the youngest in their year in the later stages of education and therefore possibly not as mature as others they learn with.

Reception classes in primary schools are usually staffed at the ratio of one teacher to twenty-five to thirty children. Infants' teachers are not always trained for work with the under fives, whose needs and stage of development are distinctly different from five and six-year-olds. Infants' classes do not normally have the space or the equipment that a nursery group would be expected to provide for four-year-olds, nor is the playspace in a primary school always arranged so that very young children are separated from ten and eleven-year-olds. Parents offered a school place for a four-year-old should inquire whether the Local Authority has made special arrangements in terms of nursery-school standards of staffing (one to thirteen), equipment and play-space for the four-year-olds it intends to take in. And whether there will be staff, either teachers or nursery nurses, specifically trained to work with the under fives.

Children admitted to primary schools at four may be expected to conform to full-time hours, a timetable, and formal activities like assembly, PE and school dinners which make little or no allowance for their stage of development and physical maturity. If parents are worried about this they should ask about the possibility of part-time attendance until five.

The Government White Paper *Better Schools* said: 'Young children can be introduced too early to the more formal language and number skills and thus miss the essential exploratory and practical work through which a good nursery programme forms a basis for later learning.' In other words, a child can actually start school TOO soon – proper nursery education may be a much more satisfactory alternative if it is available.

Obviously the decision on whether to accept a school place at four depends very much on the maturity of the four-year-old, the pre-school alternatives available and how effectively the primary school is providing for its four-year-olds. It is by no means necessarily an easy decision to make. But parents should not be intimidated by the prevailing wisdom that an early start is always a better start. It is not necessarily so.

FOUR-YEAR-OLDS AND THE NATIONAL CURRICULUM

The provisions of the National Curriculum are not statutory until children are five. However, with so many four-year-olds being taught in infants' classes, the relevance of the new attainment targets for four-year-olds (explained in detail in Chapter 3) soon became an urgent question for primary school teachers.

The National Curriculum Council issued guidance on four-year-olds in the summer of 1989 and made it quite clear that it expected the National Curriculum to affect younger children as and when it was appropriate. The question parents will want answered is precisely when that is. And the answer, as so often, cannot be precise because all children – and particularly very young children – develop at different rates and so must be treated differently.

What the NCC stresses in its advice is that there should be continuity between the education offered to four-year-olds and that offered to five-year-olds, whether they are being taught in infants' classes alongside older children or separately. There should not be artificial boundaries between the two. This does not mean that four-year-olds should be treated exactly as five-year-olds are. The NCC accepts that their needs are different and that adequate resources should be provided for a genuinely different curriculum for younger children, even though parts of it fit in neatly with the core and foundation subjects which will be taught later.

Very many nursery-age activities are concerned, for instance, with the development of language (English) and with sharing, sorting and observing – which lead on to maths and science later. Art, music and physical education all have a clear part in nursery education too, and will be part of the National Curriculum at five.

Even so, the NCC advises, some of the things four-year-olds do, either in an infants' class or a nursery school, already correspond to some of the attainment targets of the National Curriculum. For instance, amongst the English attainment targets at Level 1;

children should be able to listen attentively to poems and stories, they should be able to follow simple verbal instructions, and they should begin to recognize individual words or letters in familiar contexts. Similarly, in science, children should know that there is a wide variety of living things, which includes human beings. And in maths: children should be able to order and compare objects without measuring and understand appropriate language such as long, longer than, longest, tall, taller than, tallest, etc. Some children will reach these targets at four, others will need more time. Without distorting the normal under-five curriculum, based on exploration and imaginative play, teachers should at least be aware of where children's development is heading in National Curriculum terms.

To make continuity easy, the NCC would like to see nursery teachers in schools regarded as full members of the teaching team, and, where necessary, greater contact between nursery schools in an area and the primary school which children will move on to at five. Teachers, the NCC says, should be aware of how what they do will fit into the subsequent requirements of the National Curriculum.

3

THE PRIMARY YEARS

WHY GET INVOLVED?

Educational research is often difficult for parents – and even some teachers – to get to grips with. But ever since the Plowden Report on Primary Education, published in 1968, one research result has been widely marked and accepted: children learn better if there is a close partnership between home and school. How parents can get involved obviously varies from family to family: working parents have less opportunity than those who are not working to take part in school activities during the daytime. But even the busiest parent should recognize that their attitude – the interest and encouragement they show, and the support they give, even at a distance – can be crucial to children's progress.

What follows is a brief guide to what is going on in primary schools now, and how parents can help their children get the best out of the early years of education.

PREPARING FOR SCHOOL

Children who have had some pre-school experience in nursery class or playgroup obviously reach the age of five, and the first term of primary school, at a distinct advantage in all the social skills they will need at school. But even if children have been at home full-time before school, there are still lots of skills which parents can help them acquire.

The first day at school is a milestone in every child's life – and can be overwhelming. The teacher is likely to be a relative stranger, the other children may not all be familiar, and the numbers in the class will almost inevitably be much greater than in any nursery group the child may have attended previously. On top of all that, separation from Mother, even for a child with some pre-school experience, can still be pretty overwhelming at five. So parents can make sure that children about to start school have, if possible, the opportunity to visit, to meet the reception class teacher, and get used to the idea that when the starting age is reached, 'big' children will have an exciting and interesting time in school. There are a few practical things to be done too.

Make sure that even the most reserved children are used to the company of other children – even if that means a bit of an effort to get a child together with friends in the neighbourhood on a regular basis.

See that children can cope with the lavatory, hand-washing, and the putting on and taking off of coats and shoes on their own. Reception class teachers often have no help when children get ready to go outside to play, or have to change for PE. Buy plimsolls, and if possible shoes, without laces, and coats and sweaters that do not have too many buttons. Ensure that even children relatively reluctant to talk can make their basic needs understood. Many a puddle on a reception class floor has been caused because a child is too embarrassed to ask to go to the lavatory when it is necessary.

It all sound like common-sense but there are parents who do not take this sort of trouble, and whose children, as a result, take longer than necessary to settle down in primary school.

The second essential in a good home-school relation-ship is a confident and friendly relationship between parents and teachers. Most primary teachers these days are readily available for consultation whenever a problem arises, and many will chat to parents collecting their children almost on a day-to day basis. More serious, or less immediately personal problems – for instance over matters of school policy – should be taken up with the head-teacher.

INFORMATION FOR PARENTS

All State schools are required to produce a prospectus for parents – and most private schools do the same. The prospectus must include details of the school staff and governors, including the parent-governors elected at four-yearly intervals, and include a description of the school curriculum. Since the passing of the 1988 Education Act, the primary school curriculum is centrally defined and must include English, maths and science – three subjects which must take up a 'majority' of school time – plus technology, history and geography, art and music, and religious education. These subjects do not have to be taught separately necessarily but they must be there in some form: the common primary school practice of integrating subjects which are related is expected to continue after the full implementation of the Act, but the National Curriculum Council is gradually laying down programmes of study and assessment targets for all children from the ages of five to eleven in primary schools, starting with the youngest children.

The Act also confirmed that a religious act of worship, mainly Christian in character, should take place daily, and there should be religious education for all children except those whose parents ask for them to opt out on conscientious grounds.

NATIONAL ASSESSMENT

The 1988 Education Act provides for the assessment of all children at the age of seven and eleven. Publication of the aggregate results of tests by class and by school will take place for the older age groups, but will be at the discretion of the school for seven-year-olds, although the

Department of Education and Science has 'strongly recommended' that these results should be published too. Parents will be informed how their own child has performed, but comparison with other children in the class will not be made. The whole aim of the assessment system is to enable schools to check on progress at regular intervals, increase the amount of information available to parents on their children's progress, and enable head-teachers to offer special help to children who are either falling behind their peers, or who are so far ahead that they too need special help or facilities. Annual reports must be provided from 1991, giving details of performance in the various aspects of National Curriculum subjects.

The tests will not be of the traditional pass/fail, pencil and paper kind. Assessment, particularly for the youngest children, will be carried out during normal classroom activities by the teachers and only moderated outside the school so that standards can be set and compared. As can be seen from the attainment targets for the individual subjects, summarized later in this chapter, most assessment of young children can be carried out as a normal part of classroom procedure. What will be needed in some schools is far more detailed record-keeping if children's progress is to be monitored as closely as the law now requires.

The expert report commissioned by the Government on testing recommended a ten-point scale of achievement for children between the ages of five and sixteen, when the GCSE is normally taken. Seven-year-olds of average ability will be expected to have reached Level 2 when they are tested. Children who reach only Level 1 may require additional help: children who learn more quickly than the average may reach Level 3 at seven. Levels 4 to 10 will be the equivalent of GCSE grades.

There is no provision in the Act for parents to opt their

children out of the testing system if they object to it. Children with special educational needs may be exempted temporarily with the agreement of the head and the governors of a school. Private schools are only advised, not obliged, to follow the National Curriculum.

CAN SCHOOLS IMPLEMENT THE ACT?

Governments can legislate for what goes on in schools, but the implementation of legislation in the end comes down to the head-teacher and staff in an individual school. And there are aspects of the 1988 Act which are causing primary head-teachers some worry. Surveys show that most primary schools already spend a great deal of their time on the basic subjects of English and maths – the old three Rs. The new Act places science on a par with these essential subjects, along with technology. This could cause problems because few primary trained teachers have many skills in these areas. A programme of in-service training is helping primary teachers catch up in these newer areas of the curriculum, and in the new computer technology which goes with them, but this will take time. In the meantime the schools have to cope as best they can.

LEARNING TO READ

Many children come home after their first day at school complaining that they have not learned to read yet! Parents are not much less patient when they complain about lack of progress within a few weeks. Learning to read is never an overnight process, and it depends very much on how ready a child is to tackle reading when he or she starts school. A child whose home language is not English may need extra help with the spoken language before beginning to read and write. A child who has never seen a book before will be a lot slower getting the hang of reading than one who has been brought up with lots of picture and story-books around, and who has been read and sung to from an early age. So there are lots of things parents can do at home to help a child with early reading skills. And the help should not stop when school starts. The whole process is still a partnership in which parents have a vital role to play.

HOW TO HELP

Before four or five-year-old children learn to read, they must have developed an adequate spoken vocabulary, much of which they will have acquired at home. So, as mentioned earlier, talking to young children is of vital importance: answer their questions, however repetitive they are, and encourage conversation and children's natural curiosity about everything that is going on around them. Make sure they extend their vocabulary by learning the names of whole groups of things they may not necessarily come across every day: the more sophisticated colours, if they have a good grasp of the basic set, zoo and farm animals, common flowers and birds, the various parts of the car or bus they travel in regularly, and so on. Picture-books help, but so does a wide experience of activities outside the home, even if it consists of just visits to the local park, library or museum which cost very little but provide lots of opportunity for conversation.

Listening is important too because learning to read depends on good discrimination between sounds. Children love having stories read to them, and it is an activity which should not stop just because they are beginning to be able to read for themselves. A story read aloud will be several stages of difficulty ahead of what the average five or six-year-old can read, and so will still be useful for developing vocabulary, a grasp of more complex grammatical structures, and attention. But it should not be a chore: it should be fun, and poetry and the old nursery rhymes are useful ways of keeping it fun. As mentioned earlier, there is some research which indicates that the simple rhymes and rhythms of nursery rhymes help children to develop good auditory dis-crimination, which helps with reading.

Once at school, some time will be spent on developing pre-reading skills like the recognition of shapes and sounds, matching and sorting games. Words will probably be introduced through flash cards, and by helping children to write what they want to say on their paintings or on labels. All this can be backed up at home with similar games. The school's system of labelling familiar objects can easily be extended, so that children become familiar with the look of common words like door, table, chair, and, of course, their own name.

READING SCHEMES

Once the early stages of learning to read are over, most primary schools will make use of a reading scheme: a graded set of books which take children steadily through from one level of difficulty to the next. A fast learner might move very quickly from one level to the next, skipping books along the way. A slow learner may need the extra practice which is entailed in reading every book on a certain level before moving on. It is question of the teacher's judgement.

There are some schools which prefer to use a selection of children's books to supplement their reading scheme, or even to replace it altogether. In that case they usually grade the level of difficulty of the available books – probably by the use of a colour code – so that teachers and parents can still be sure that children are moving steadily towards more difficult reading matter. There is nothing unusual, though, in children continuing to read books that are technically 'too easy' for some of the time, at school or at home. Some children find satisfaction and extra security in being able to skim through a familiar book quickly. There is nothing wrong with that so long as progress continues to be made and measured towards more difficult texts.

Some schools also use other materials to help with early reading. 'Breakthrough to Literacy' is sometimes found in infants classes. This consists of a large wallet containing a large selection of word cards which children can select to make into sentences, so effectively creating their own reading materials, and integrating the learning of reading and writing.

HOME SCHOOL READING PARTNERSHIPS

There is now a lot of evidence from experimental schemes that children's reading improves dramatically if parents are involved in the teaching process as well as teachers. The most common type of scheme now being adopted by primary schools involves the family agreeing to read with a child for a certain number of short periods a week at home. The school will explain to the parents just how they want this done – a lot of heavy-handed correction of mistakes is often self-defeating because it destroys children's confidence. The usual advice is that mistakes should simply be corrected once, without great drama, and then the reading allowed to continue. The results of such schemes can be dramatic, with a six to nine month rise in reading age reported in one survey of a brief nine-week scheme. And the improvement remained even when the scheme ended. Children themselves believed that they had become better readers, and that they enjoyed reading more, at the end of the experiment.

LEARNING TO WRITE

Very young children will be delighted to scribble with a crayon. If that early activity is encouraged they will absorb the idea that writing is a desirable and enjoyable activity and will not be too daunted when the learning process becomes formalized in the infants' class or school. By the time they arrive at school they may already be able to make an attempt at writing their name – or at least be able to add a kiss to the bottom of a card or letter to Granny or some other member of the family. But none of this early enthusiasm for making marks on paper means that learning to write is an easy process. In fact it is a learning process which never actually finishes: even the most distinguished novelists or speech writers may still occasionally have to search for just the right word to express their meaning.

So it is not just a question of mechanically learning to handle shapes and put the correct marks on paper, though for many young children that is difficult enough, involving as it does the co-ordination of hand, brain and eye which does not always come easily at five or six. It is not even a question of learning to spell the highly irregular English language correctly. It is a complex process which not only starts at the mechanical stage of forming letters and words on paper, but goes on to involve the ordering of ideas, the selection of what to say and the best way to say it, putting the words down, and revising, editing and then completing the piece of writing produced. And when you think about what that piece of writing might be: a poem, a report, a letter, an advertisement, a set of instructions, a bill, a complaint, or a play, then it gives some indication of the task ahead of the infant teacher faced with a class of thirty children who do not know a letter from a sentence at the beginning of their school career.

The good primary school will try to introduce children to all the various kinds of writing they will need in later life, not neglecting the imaginative writing, both poetry and prose, which so many people give up once school days are over. And they will be aware, as most parents are, of the need to encourage children to write correct, intelligible English, and at the same time time to allow, in the right circumstances, their imagination full rein.

Parents can help in the process of acquiring writing skills just as much as they can with reading. It is a good idea to give even quite young children a place where they can write in comfort, a small desk, and their own paper, pencils and pens. And it should not be too difficult to allow children the chance to use their writing as part and parcel of family life – keeping the grocery list up to date, taking down messages, copying out poems or songs that particularly appeal to one member of the family or another, keeping a diary. As the educationist Margaret Meek puts it, reading and writing both come eventually through practice, persistence and pleasure.

ATTAINMENT IN ENGLISH

The committee chaired by Professor Brian Cox which drew up attainment targets for five to eleven-year-olds in 1988 was the subject of much controversy. The teaching of English in schools had been the subject of great criticism on the grounds that traditional teaching of spelling, grammar and standard English had been neglected. When the committee's report was published, it was clear that the experts had rejected the more polarized views of English teaching, and come down in favour of a consensus which, they argued, more closely reflected what was already happening in good primary schools.

The committee identified five main aims for English in the curriculum: it should:

(a) Encourage personal growth by developing children's imaginative and aesthetic lives.
(b) Prepare them for adult life and the day-to-day

39

demands of the spoken and printed word.

(c) Promote a cross curricular view to help with the use of language in all subjects.

(d) Nurture an appreciation of a cultural heritage and those works of literature that are amongst the finest in the language.

(e) Emphasize the importance of a critical understanding of the world and the meanings conveyed in the newspaper and other media.

On the thorny question of formal grammar teaching they recommended that children should be taught to understand the structure of the language and how it works, something which most primary teachers accepted as a matter of course. This did not mean that children needed to be introduced to inappropriate Latinate grammatical exercises. There should be no return to drills and sentence parsing.

The committee also stated that all schools have the responsibility to teach all children 'standard English' even if this is not the language or the dialect which they use at home. Without access to standard English, the committee said, children would find that many areas of importance were closed to them in later life, in industry and commerce, cultural activities and further and higher education. But standard English is not static, they warned: it is itself a form of the language which is changing, and one which can be used badly just as much as any dialect.

ATTAINMENT TARGETS IN ENGLISH

The National Curriculum requirements for English, based on the Cox Report, set out attainment targets for two distinct aspects of reading – comprehension and understanding on the one hand, and the use of reading for information retrieval on the other. The target attainments assume that an average seven-year-old should be capable of Level 2, and an average eleven-year-old of Level 4.

ATTAINMENT TARGETS FOR READING

The following targets should indicate the development of the ability to read, understand and respond to all types of writing.

Pupils should be able to:

Level 1
(a) Recognize that print conveys meaning, in books and in other forms in the everyday world.
(b) Show signs of developing an interest in books (e.g. by turning to them readily, looking at and talking about them).
(c) Begin to recognize individual words or letters in familiar contexts.
(d) Talk in simple terms about the content of stories, or information in non-fiction books.

Level 2
(a) Read accurately and understand straightforward signs, labels and notices.
(b) Demonstrate knowledge of the alphabet in using word books and simple dictionaries.
(c) Use picture and context cues: words recognized on sight and phonic cues in reading.
(d) Describe what has happened in a story and predict what may happen next.
(e) Listen and respond to stories, poems and other material read aloud, expressing opinions informed by what has been read.
(f) Read a range of material with some independence, accuracy, fluency and understanding.

Level 3
(a) Read silently and with sustained concentration.
(b) Read aloud from familiar stories and poems, fluently and with appropriate expression.
(c) Listen attentively to stories, talk about story-line, characters, and significant details.
(d) Revise a clear set of questions that will enable them to select and use information sources and reference books.
(e) Demonstrate, in talking about stories and poems, that they are beginning to use inference, deduction and previous reading experience to find and appreciate meanings beyond the literal.
(f) Bring to their writing and discussion about stories some understanding of the way stories are structured.

Level 4 (only recommended so far)
(a) Read regularly over a widening range of prose and verse.
(b) Give reasons for establishing preferences.
(c) Draw on reading experience to make comparisons and note parallels.
(d) Show a developing familiarity with a number of basic kinds of narrative (children's fiction, legend, fable, folk-tale, fantasy, science fiction, etc.).
(e) Read aloud with increasing confidence and fluency from a range of familiar literature with appropriate expression.
(f) Discuss aspects of a variety of books and poems in some detail, expressing opinions and providing supporting evidence from the text.

Level 5
(a) Read regularly and voluntarily over an even wider range of prose and verse.
(b) Show developing tastes and preferences over an increasing range of material.

(c) Display fluency, adaptability and accuracy when deploying a range of reading strategies, whether reading to themselves or aloud.

(d) Show through discussion that they can use text to infer, deduce, predict, compare and evaluate.

ATTAINMENT TARGETS FOR WRITING

Pupils should be able to:

Level 1

Use pictures, symbols or isolated letters, words or phrases to communicate meaning.

Level 2

(a) Produce independently pieces of writing using complete sentences, some of them demarcated with capital letters and full-stops.

(b) Structure sequences of real or imagined events coherently in chronological accounts.

(c) Write stories showing an understanding of the rudiments of story structure by establishing an opening, characters and one or more events.

(d) Produce simple coherent non-chronological writing.

Level 3

(a) Produce, independently, pieces of writing using complete sentences, mainly demarcated with capital letters and full stops or question marks.

(b) Shape chronological writing, beginning to use a wider range of sentence connectives than 'and' and 'then'.

(c) Write more complex stories with detail beyond simple events and with a defined ending.

(d) Produce a range of types of non-chronological writing.

(e) Begin to revise and redraft in discussion with the teacher, other adults, or other children in the class, paying attention to meaning and clarity as well as checking for matters such as correct and consistent use of tenses and pronouns.

Level 4 (only recommended so far)
(a) Produce well-structured narratives with an opening, a setting, characters, a series of events and a resolution.
(b) Organize in a logical way non-chronological writing (e.g. description, explanation, argument for a point of view).
(c) Use lay-out, sub-headings, paragraphing, verse structure, etc to organize different kinds of text.
(d) Use sentence structures which show some differentiations from the forms characteristic of speech (e.g. a wider range of sentence connectives than the 'and' and 'then' typical of speech; a wider range of subordinate clauses; expanded noun phrases).
(e) Use written standard English where appropriate.
(f) Demarcate most sentences with capital letters and full stops or question marks.
(g) Use a widening range of devices which organize a text (such as inverted commas, apostrophes, commas and exclamations marks).
(h) Revise and redraft independently.
(i) Discuss the organization of their own writing.

Level 5
(a) Attempt to produce impersonal writing when required.
(b) Choose to use stylistic effects (such as the alteration of word order for emphasis).
(c) Use ellipses and other constructions that reduce repetition.
(d) Discuss stylistic effects (e.g. choice of vocabulary) aimed for in their own writing.

ATTAINMENT TARGETS FOR HANDWRITING
Pupils should be able to:

Level 1
Begin to form letters but with little physical control over the size, shape and/or orientation of letters or lines of writing.

Level 2
(a) Produce legible upper and lower case letters in one style (e.g. printed) and use them consistently (i.e. not randomly mixed within words).
(b) Produce letters that are visibly formed and properly oriented and that have clear ascenders and descenders where necessary.

Level 3
Begin to produce a clear and legible cursive (joined-up) writing.

Level 4 (only recommended so far)
Produce a more fluent cursive style in independent work.

Level 5
Produce clear and legible handwriting in both printed and cursive styles.

ATTAINMENT TARGETS FOR SPELLING
Pupils should be able to:

Level 1
(a) Begin to show an understanding of the difference between drawing and writing and between numbers and letters.
(b) Use at least single letters or pairs of letters to represent whole words or parts of words.
(c) Write some letter shapes in response to speech sounds and letter names.

Level 2
(a) Produce recognizable (though not necessarily always correct) spellings of a range of common sight words.
(b) Spell correctly monosyllabic words which observe common patterns in their own writing.
(c) Use these principles also to attempt the spelling of a wider range of words.
(d) Show knowledge of the names and order of the letters of the alphabet.

Level 3
(a) Spell correctly frequent polysyllabic words which observe common patterns in their own writing.
(b) Recognize and use correctly regular patterns for vowel sounds and common letter strings.
(c) Show a growing awareness of word families and their relationships.
(d) Begin to check spelling when revising and redrafting work.

Level 4 (only recommended so far)
Spell correctly words which display the other main patterns in English spelling, including the main prefixes and suffixes.

Level 5
Spell correctly words of increasing complexity, including words with inflexional suffixes (e.g. --ed, --ing), consonant doubling, etc., and words where the spelling highlights semantic relationships (e.g. sign, signature).

ATTAINMENT TARGETS FOR SPEAKING AND LISTENING
Pupils should be able to:

Level 1
(a) Speak freely and listen in group activities and imaginative play.

(b) Respond to simple classroom instructions given by a teacher.

(c) Listen attentively and respond to stories and poems.

Level 2

(a) Speak and listen as a member of a group engaged in a task.

(b) Listen attentively and respond to stories and poetry, and talk about them.

(c) Speak freely to the teacher, ask and answer questions.

(d) Respond to an increasing range and complexity of instructions given by a teacher, and give simple instructions.

(e) Describe an event, real or imagined, to the teacher or another pupil.

Level 3

(a) Relate real or imaginary events in a connected narrative which conveys meaning to a group of pupils, the teacher or another known adult.

(b) Convey accurately a simple message.

(c) Give and receive and follow accurately precise instructions when pursuing a task individually or as a member of a group.

(d) Listen with an increased span of concentration to other children and adults, asking and responding to questions and commenting on what has been said.

Level 4 (only recommended so far)

(a) Describe an event or experience to a group of peers, clearly, audibly and in detail.

(b) Give and receive precise instructions and follow them.

(c) Ask relevant questions with increasing confidence.

(d) Offer a reasoned explanation of how a task has been done or a problem has been solved.

(e) Take part effectively in a small group discussion and respond to others in the group.
(f) Make confident use of the telephone.
(g) Speak freely and audibly to a class.
(h) Speak freely and audibly to the adults encountered in school.

Level 5
(a) Speak freely and audibly to a larger audience of peers and adults.
(b) Discuss and debate constructively, advocating and justifying a particular point of view.
(c) Contribute effectively to a small group discussion which aims to reach agreement on a given assignment.

PRIMARY LANGUAGE RECORDS

One of the Cox Report's other recommendations was that children's progress in English should be monitored by the introduction of a common national system of record-keeping. The model they recommended was developed by the Inner London Education Authority in its primary schools and enabled schools to keep an accurate long-term record of children's progress in reading, writing, speaking and listening from their first term at school. The ILEA record, now adopted by other authorities, is passed up the school system with a child, and its results are used to advise parents on children's progress.

MATHS

Parents often worry as much about their children's maths as they do about their reading skills, and their worry is compounded because teaching methods may appear to have changed since they themselves were at school. In fact 'modern maths', which is not so modern any longer, starts from the premise that children will not learn unless they understand, a premise that has a lot of psychological backing, and in maths understanding is perhaps more important than in any other area of the school curriculum.

Parents often do not realize how different a young child's concept of number is from that of an adult. If you ask a four-year-old, for instance, to count six pencils, she may do so correctly. It you jumble them up and ask her to count again, though, she may not be immediately sure of the answer even though it is obvious that you have not moved any of the group, or added another. The fact that numbers remain the same, although they may be arranged differently, is one which children learn from experience. Or they may insist that there are more hippopotamuses in a picture than mice, simply because the hippos are bigger. In other words, mathematical concepts that we take for granted, may not be at all obvious to small children. They have to be learned. And much of the early mathematical work in reception classes – some of which may look like 'playing' – is devoted to helping children understand some of these basic principles.

Modern primary schools also start with the enormous advantage that they do not have to teach children a lot of the arithmetical manipulation which the older generations had to contend with. Feet and inches, rods and perches, as well as pounds, shillings and pence have all mercifully been confined to the dustbin of history, which has left room in the primary curriculum for a lot of mathematical teaching which was not reached until secondary school level twenty years ago. So paradoxically primary maths has become easier and harder at the same time. And this may lead to a lot of confusion between home and school.

There are also calculators, to which most adults who use maths in their everyday life – whether they are accountants or engineers or research scientists – turn automatically. Children will be introduced to the use of calculators during their school careers as an essential tool: the only dispute in schools is the right point at which to make them available, and how firm a grasp of the basic arithmetical procedures children should have before they turn to electronic help for the actual calculations. Is it, for instance, necessary to be able to work out long-division on paper rather than by using a calculator? Most professional maths teachers think not, so long as the principle of division is firmly understood. Some politicians disagree, and when the attainment targets for the National Curriculum were published, pencil and paper long-division found a place there, in spite of widespread professional reservations.

Parents are also sometimes taken by surprise by the amount of practical work which takes place in maths these days. Again, the aim is to encourage children's grasp of basic principles rather than drilling them in paper and pencil 'sums' which may not make much sense in practical situations. Many children, for instance, can do sums involving hundreds and tens, but cannot say how many ten pence pieces they should get for 67p. The understanding of the relationship between tens, hundreds and larger units only comes from the experience of assembling concrete things into groups of ten, or a hundred. It may look like a game, but leads to genuine understanding of mathematical principles.

Children are now encouraged to discover and test out rules and relationships between numbers. This leads onto the setting up of mathematical problems and investigations. The starting point may be a simple problem or puzzle: how many ways can you arrange nine objects on a square tray, or what amounts can you make up using only two and ten pence coins? There may not be a single 'right' answer: there may be many. The aim is to encourage children to think in mathematical terms, and incidentally reveal any weaknesses in their own mathematical logic which the teacher can then try to strengthen.

Parents can support children's mathematical learning at home by being aware right from the pre-school stage of the use they make of maths in everyday life. There are plenty of number games and rhymes even for toddlers. Children who are big enough to lay the table can be encouraged to count out the spoons and forks. Much primary school maths includes practical work, so it helps if older children can help to weigh ingredients for recipes, or measure up for do-it-yourself tasks about the house, and use family situations, television and books, to explore concepts like probability, size, weight, velocity, acceleration and height. Maths is after all to a large extent about how the world works all around us.

It is particularly important for parents with daughters to give some encouragement at home. Girls traditionally do well in maths as calculation in primary schools: less well than boys when they move up to secondary schools where maths branches out into the solving of problems, measuring, ratio and spatial ideas. And boys' facility in these areas seems to come to a large extent from their experience in the real world of construction kits, an obsession with 'taking things apart to see how they work', riding and maintaining bikes, and vigorous outdoor activities. Yet in a world increasingly dominated by mathematical ideas it is just as important for girls to succeed to a high level as it is for their brothers. Parents should avoid encouraging girls in the idea that this is in any way a male subject, or that it is normal for girls not to do well. It isn't. And the family's attitude, and particularly the mother's, may be crucial in helping girls to reach their full potential in a vital subject.

51

NATIONAL CURRICULUM MATHS

The National Curriculum specifies a set of fourteen attainment targets which describe the sort of work which children of all ages should be covering in maths. These are:

1. Using and applying mathematics: using number, algebra and measures in practical tasks and real life problems.
2. Number: understanding number and number notation.
3. Number: understanding number operations (addition, subtraction, multiplication and division) and making use of appropriate methods of calculation.
4. Number: estimating and approximating in number.
5. Number/algebra: recognizing and using patterns, relationships and sequences, and making generalizations.
6. Algebra: recognizing and using functions, formulae, equations and inequalities.
7. Algebra: using graphical representation of algebraic functions.
8. Measures: estimating and measuring quantities and appreciating the approximate nature of measurement.
9. Using and applying mathematics: using shape and space and handling data in practical tasks and real life problems, and within mathematics itself.
10. Shape and space: recognizing and using the properties of two dimensional and three dimensional shapes.
11. Shape and space: recognizing location and using transformation in the study of space.
12. Handling data: collecting, recording and processing data.
13. Handling data: representing and interpreting data.

14. Handling data: understanding, estimating and calculating probabilities.

Some of these attainment goals may seem pretty remote from the average five-year-old just starting school: but even quite young children will quickly be introduced to most of the topics which span the fourteen goals: number, most obviously, but also measurement, shape and space, the simple handling of data in the drawing up of graphs (how many children in the class have blue eyes, grey eyes or brown eyes, for instance, or what is the average height of the boys and the girls). And even algebra will usually be introduced by the age of eleven.

Even so, some specific examples from the National Curriculum Council's recommendations give a clearer idea of what primary school children will be expected to achieve at the different levels of attainment in the fourteen areas of the mathematics curriculum.

Within the scope of attainment target 2 above: understanding number and number notation, an average five-year-old reaching Level 1 should be able to:

(a) Count, read, write and order numbers to at least 10, and know that the size of a set is given by the last number in the count: i.e. if you count six pencils one, two, three, etc. the total is six.

(b) Understand the conservation of number: e.g. show that if a set of eight pens is counted twice in different orders the answer will be the same.

An average seven-year-old reaching Level 2 should be able to:

(a) Read, write and order numbers to at least 100 and use the knowledge that the tens digit indicate the number of tens: e.g. know (without counting in order) that $30 + 7$ is 37; 10 more than 42 is 52; and $3 \times 10p$ coins and $2 \times 2p$ coins give 34p.

(b) Understand the meaning of 'a half' and 'a quarter': e.g. find a quarter of a piece of string; know that half of 8 is 4.

An average nine-year-old reaching Level 3 should be able to:

(a) Read, write and order numbers to at least 1,000, and use the knowledge that the position of a digit indicates its value: e.g. know that four hundred and two is written 402 and why neither 42 nor 4002 is correct.
(b) Use decimal notation as the conventional way of recording in money: e.g. know that 3 x £1 coins plus 3 x 2p coins is written as £3.06 and that 3.6 on a calculator means £3.60 in the context of money.
(c) Appreciate the meaning of negative whole numbers: e.g. read a temperature scale; understand a negative output on a calculator.

An average eleven-year-old reaching Level 4 should be able to:

(a) Read, write and order whole numbers. Understand the effect of multiplying a whole number by 10 or 100: e.g. explain why the cost of ten objects costing £23 each is £230.
(b) Understand and use decimal notation to two decimal places in the context of measurement: e.g. read scales marked in hundredths and numbered in tenths (1.89m).
(c) Recognize and understand simple everyday fractions: e.g. estimate ¾ of the length of a piece of wood or ⅓ of a pint of milk (in baking).
(d) Recognize and understand everyday percentages: e.g. examine attendance rates at school during a period of time.

(e) Understand and use the relation between place values in whole numbers: e.g. know that 5,000 is 5 thousands or 50 hundreds or 500 tens or 5,000 ones.

SCIENCE AND TECHNOLOGY

This is the area of the National Curriculum which many primary teachers will find the hardest to implement. Very few primary teachers have included science or technology as part of their initial training, and although there has been a rapid expansion in scientific work in primary schools in recent years, many are perhaps justifiably worried about their ability to take the brightest children up to Level 5 on the attainment targets in schools which do not have specialist staff or accommodation or equipment for science.

The first working-party report on technology as a foundation subject in all schools admitted that it would pose a challenge and that in-service training would be needed for teachers. The working party defined technology very broadly, and included aspects of the curriculum such as home economics and information technology. Detailed attainment targets are not yet available, but the report suggested that, for instance, at Level 2 the average seven-year-old should be able to store, retrieve modify and use information with the aid of a computer. At Level 4 the average eleven-year-old should be able to capture information and add it to an existing data-base, to examine retrieved information critically in order to identify any obviously aberrant items and to present retrieved information appropriately.

The full attainment targets for science and proposed targets for technology, which apply to both primary and secondary schools, appear in Chapter 10.

THE ARTS

One of the joys of the British primary school is undoubtedly the high standard of creative work achieved right across the arts, from music and drama to painting and pottery. The school curriculum enshrines the right of every child to music and art, and it is unlikely that primary school practice will change much in this area with the introduction of the National Curriculum, although some primary teachers fear that the time available for creative work may be squeezed by the emphasis on more 'academic' subjects.

Parents should beware of treating the creative areas as 'optional extras', though. Creative activities are vital to children's development and parents can help and encourage work in these areas of the curriculum at home by providing opportunities for young musicians to practise, or young artists to continue their work out of school time. And it is always as well to remember that the thrill of achievement in one area of school life can be a motivating force which will carry children through other aspects of their education which they may find much more difficult and less rewarding. A sense of pride in what is being done – whether it is a rendering of a simple tune on the recorder or the creation of a papier mâché dragon for the school pageant – is always valuable.

It is an area where parents are often asked to help in very practical ways too. Materials for creative activities are often expensive, and schools are adept at making use of all sorts of cast-off and spare bits and pieces from egg boxes and used computer paper to old clothes for 'dressing up' or more formal drama. The reward for parents will lie in the displays of creative work which make many primary schools such attractive and exciting places to visit, or at the end-of-term pantomime or concert when the children's pride and excitement in their own achievements can be shared by the whole family.

THE HUMANITIES

The National Curriculum guarantees a place for history and geography and, of course, religious education, in the primary school curriculum, but the programmes of study and attainment targets are not expected to be drawn up much before 1991. All three subjects are frequently taught by means of topics or projects, or as part of a course of integrated studies, rather than as separate items on a timetable. This does not mean that children are receiving any less of the basic subjects now laid down by law. The Department of Education and Science has said that it sees no inconsistency between integrated teaching methods and the National Curriculum.

RELIGIOUS EDUCATION

The curriculum for religious education has been since 1944, and will continue to be, drawn up by an advisory committee upon which the main religious denominations, including the non-Christian denominations, are represented. New syllabuses drawn up since the 1988 Education Act must reflect the fact that Britain is a 'mainly Christian' country but this does not rule out teaching about the other major world religions. Families have the right to withdraw their children from religious education, but in primary schools where RE may be integrated with other subjects, this can cause difficulties. Families from minority religions, or of no religion, should discuss any reservations they have over the content of RE with the school. Sympathetic teachers can usually find a way of avoiding offence to family beliefs if these are discussed in a friendly way, without the need to remove a child from the classroom entirely while religious topics are being discussed. Obviously there is a risk that young children will find complete withdrawal from their class upsetting, especially if they are the only children who are expected to leave.

HELPING IN SCHOOL

Most primary schools these days welcome parents into school as voluntary helpers. Obviously the ability of parents to volunteer varies from family to family: parents with full-time jobs should not feel guilty if they cannot find the time, but those who can spare a few hours a week will find it a rewarding and enlightening experience.

The sorts of jobs parents are asked to do fall into two categories: those that involve chores which can be undertaken apart from the teachers: running the library, assisting in the school office, or doing odd jobs of maintenance around the school fall into the first category; other schools welcome parents into classrooms to work with the teachers in direct contact with children. The latter is a more sensitive area, and when it was first proposed in the 1960s many teachers were very wary of what they regarded as a potential threat to their professional prerogatives. Parents in classrooms should be sensitive to the fact that they are guests and very much assistants to the trained teachers, if they are to avoid stepping on the toes of the professionals. Even so, enough schools have now taken on parent volunteers for it to be clear that this is something which can work very well, and to the advantage of the children, who can only gain from having extra adult attention, especially in areas where classes are relatively large.

There are a few do's and don'ts for parents to remember in school.

1. Never contradict or argue with a teacher in front of children.

2. Maintain the same level of formality in front of the children as the teachers do.

3. Do not go into the staff-room unless you are invited.

4. Do not single out your own children in any way: you will embarrass the children as well as the staff!
5. Discuss with the teachers what they expect you to do in the classroom – and what they prefer to reserve for themselves – and stick to those ground-rules.
6. If there is any problem over the children's work or over discipline which you cannot handle refer the child immediately to the teacher in charge.

ASSISTING ON OUTINGS

Schools sometimes ask parents to assist on school outings, or even to accompany school parties on visits involving nights away. Again, this can be a useful and rewarding experience provided the parent recognizes that there are responsibilities involved and that no school trip is just an outing for any of the adults who go along. They are all on duty and responsible for the children's safety unless specifically excused from that duty for a time by the party leader.

Following several tragic accidents involving school parties, the rules imposed by Local Authorities for school outings have been tightened. The ground-rules for parents follow on from the list of do's and don'ts in the classroom above. In addition, parents should be clear about:

1. Exactly who is in charge of the party – this should be one teacher, and may not necessarily be the head-teacher.
2. What the precise responsibilities of the parent volunteers are during the journey and during the different parts of a visit – sightseeing, in residential accommodation, etc.
3. What insurance cover is provided for all members of the party.

4. Which adult member of the party has responsibility
   for first-aid in the event of an accident.

4

PARENT-TEACHER ASSOCIATIONS

Most schools have a Parent-Teacher Association which can provide committed parents with a useful and constructive role in the life of a school. PTAs generally have three distinct functions: to raise funds for the school to buy optional – and sometimes these days unfortunately not so optional – extras which the Local Authority does not normally provide; to give parents and teachers the chance to get to know each other socially; and to provide a forum for staff and parents to discuss educational developments which affect their children.

Obviously PTAs vary in the weight they give to these three separate functions. At a time when many Local Authorities have been reducing educational expenditure, fund-raising has come to dominate the proceedings of many associations, to the extent that at some schools the PTA is pumping many thousands of pounds into school funds and providing basic items such as textbooks which the school could not otherwise afford. But with the pace of educational change quickening with the passing of the 1988 Education Act, it is likely that many more PTAs will develop their educational function as school staff feel the need to explain to parents in a common forum how the changes in curriculum and testing procedures are going to affect their schools over the next few years.

FUND-RAISING

For some PTAs fund-raising is, of necessity, a major activity. The most common means of fund-raising are the traditional jumble sales and fairs – Christmas and Summer – which bring people into school both to sell and to buy, to play money-raising games like guessing the weight of a cake, shying at coconuts or throwing wellies, or to exercise the national passion for gambling by buying raffle tickets for anything from a basket of fruit to a used car.

The 'sponsorship' craze has also benefited schools powerfully, with anything from sponsored runs and swims to sponsored weight-losing bringing in the loot. Some schools do well out of regular Bingo evenings, which bring in the grannies as well as parents; others, especially with more affluent catchment areas, raise most of their money by asking parents to covenant regular gifts to the school, while some fortunate private schools find they can fund new buildings, bursaries or libraries simply by appealing to old boys and girls for the cash: often with the help of professional fund-raisers who specialize in raising money for educational institutions.

PTAs these days often debate fiercely the ethics of parental funds being spent on essentials such as library books and textbooks in addition to the traditional 'extras' like video-recorders and mini-buses. Some parents believe strongly that if PTAs are tempted to provide essential items there will be less pressure on Local Authorities, and the Government, to fund schools adequately, and that in time, if parental funding remains high, the quality of education offered by schools in relatively affluent areas will far outstrip what is available in poorer neighbourhoods, so compounding existing social inequalities with educational inequities as well. It is one of those arguments where the generally accepted principle that the essentials of education should be provided free of charge in maintained schools collides with the desire of individual parents to do the best for their own children here and now: and if that means providing what is needed themselves, then so be it. The less generous the Local Authority is, the sharper the argument becomes.

SOCIAL EVENTS

Social events organized by PTAs vary according to the nature of the school's catchment area, and in schools which serve families from very varied backgrounds much thought is often given to finding entertaining activities which will attract a wide clientele. Teachers very often regard social activities as a valuable way of meeting parents who rarely come into school on other occasions. Some groups of parents may be well suited by a wine and cheese party, others might prefer a barn-dance, a hot-pot supper, a disco or a bingo evening. Schools with children from a number of ethnic minority communities have found that international evenings – with food and musical entertainment provided by members of the different communities – are a good way to bring a wide range of families together.

EDUCATIONAL ACTIVITIES

The pace of educational change is accelerating, and some of the best attended meetings organized by PTAs over the last few years have been to explain the new GCSE examination, the Technical and Vocational Education Initiative (TVEI) now being extended to all maintained secondary schools, and records of achievement also being introduced in secondary schools. In primary schools, talks and workshops – allowing parents some 'hands on' experience of the curriculum – on the teaching of reading, modern maths teaching, and the use of computers – have proved popular. There is no doubt that the introduction of the National Curriculum and the new testing procedures for children at seven, eleven and fourteen, will lead most schools to organize parents' evenings at which staff and outside experts can explain how the changes will affect pupils. Not many parents or young people have yet realized that 'options' at fourteen, when pupils have traditionally given up some subjects, will be greatly restricted by the National Curriculum.

Not all PTAs avoid 'political' issues, although most are precluded by their constitutions from taking a party political stance. This does not prevent them from arranging meetings to discuss issues of local or national educational politics, such as school re-organization, the possibility of 'opting out', the educational issues at stake in local or national elections, or the likely effects of new legislation, so long as the speakers include represent-atives of all the political parties in contention.

Some PTAs have gone further than the 'one off' educational meeting, by arranging series of lectures or discussions on relevant topics, in conjunction with local adult education organizers. Some financial help may be available for this more formal kind of educational activity.

WHO RUNS THE PTA?

The constitution of the PTA varies from school to school. Some provide for the head-teacher to chair the association: others insist on a non-teacher chairperson. All will be administered by a committee, with a clerk or secretary responsible for the drawing up of the agenda, the keeping of minutes and the convening of meetings, and a treasurer who takes the heavy responsibility of looking after the PTA funds and managing its sometimes large bank account.

Every PTA will hold an annual general meeting at which the officers will report on the previous year's activities and a new committee will be elected – if there is any competition for places – to run the association for the following year. Committee meetings may be private, or open to all members. All parents of children at the school, and school teaching staff, are normally automatically members of the PTA. Agendas and minutes of committee meetings are usually made available to parents either individually or on a special noticeboard in school. It is usual for the school office to handle PTA notices which are to be distributed by the children, but for the PTA to pay for its own stationery and other expenses.

Some PTA committees receive a regular report from the head-teacher and from parent-governors, who in many instances are parents who have already held office on the PTA committee. There is no legal requirement for parent-governors to report back to other parents in this way, and some parts of the agenda at governors' meetings are confidential. But as governors' minutes must be made available to parents if they request them, an informal report is one way of making what is in any case legally accessible to interested parents, even more accessible.

In some schools the head-teacher hands over responsibility for the organization of parent-governor elections to the PTA, which may either circulate brief manifestos from the candidates to all parents along with ballot papers, or arrange a meeting at which candidates can speak directly to their electors. The ballot, however, must still be 'postal', i.e. delivered home by pupils and returned to school by hand or post.

Some head-teachers dislike Parent-Teacher Associations on the grounds that they are sometimes taken over by a self-selecting group of usually articulate parents, who make other less confident parents feel unwanted and excluded from their activities. Inevitably elected PTA officers will be people who have the time and energy to take on the organizational tasks involved and attend meetings regularly. But a PTA should never be allowed to become an exclusive club for a few, or a divisive rather than a constructive force within a school. The annual general meeting should be used to make sure that people are elected to the committee who are as representative of the whole school community as possible, and some practical help – for instance, with baby-sitting if committee meetings are held in the evening – might make it possible for wider range of parents to stand for office.

HOW TO START A PTA

It is not possible to establish a PTA without the consent of the head-teacher, if school staff are to be included in membership. If a head-teacher is adamantly opposed to the idea of a PTA, there is nothing to stop parents alone forming some similar association of 'friends of the school' to which they could invite sympathetic members of staff as guests, and which could serve many of the functions of a PTA, including fund-raising for the school. But clearly it is much more satisfactory to run an organization which is dedicated to improving home-school links with the support of the head than without it. So some patient negotiation might be preferable to rushing in.

Information about setting up a new PTA or parents' group can be obtained from the National Confederation of PTAs, an organization which offers advice and help to 6,000 individual school associations, and 40 federations of PTAs in Local Education Authority areas. It publishes a regular magazine, *Home and School*, for members, advises on insurance for PTA functions, and, through its annual conference of affiliated associations, discusses policy issues of concern to parents and acts as a pressure group on their behalf.

The NCPTA stands at the apex of the home-school movement, is consulted widely on educational issues – and vigorously puts forward its own point of view, as defined at its annual conference, as the most representative national body of parents. At local level area federations of PTAs also represent parental views in discussions with Local Authorities, and local branches of political parties in debates on educational policy. Some federations of PTAs have instituted regular discussion meetings with chief education officers, or political leaders, to make sure that the parental voice is heard.

TAKING PROBLEMS TO THE PTA

The PTA is not the forum for the discussion of the problems of individual children, or complaints about individual teachers. These are most appropriately dealt with through the head-teacher, and if that fails to resolve an issue, through the school governors, either using the parent-governors as a channel of communication, or by writing direct to the chairperson and asking for the matter to be raised.

PTA committees, though, are a useful forum for the discussion of general issues of school policy, or difficulty, upon which there might be a constructive exchange of views between parents and staff. Grievances are much better aired frankly there than fomented in discussion at the school gate.

5

PARENT-GOVERNORS

Shouldn't you become a school governor? The question comes direct from the Department of Education and Science in a recruiting leaflet issued in 1988, just as the Conservative Government's major new Education Act was passing through Parliament. That Act gave school governors in England and Wales substantial new powers: for the first time almost all of them were to be given control of school finances (the possible exception being the smaller primary schools with less than 200 pupils); and governors would have the entirely new right to begin the procedures to take a school out of Local Authority control, to 'opt out', as the politicians put it. Power indeed!

The idea that parents should play some part in school management – as opposed to simply co-operating with teachers in the education of their own children – first surfaced in the 1970s. At a time when some Local Authorities like Sheffield were already beginning to recruit parents to governing bodies, the Taylor Committee, set up by the then Labour Government, recommended that school governors should be equally divided between elected parent and teacher represent-atives, nominees of the Local Education Authority, who until that time had dominated school management, and co-opted representatives of the local community around a school.

The Taylor Report was pretty warmly welcomed – although there were local politicians of all persuasions who did not much like the idea of handing over control of schools to non-politicians. But when the Conservatives came to power in 1979 they immediately set about implementing a watered-down version of the Taylor Report: they drew the line at giving teachers equal representation with parents, but all schools were to have individual governing bodies with elected parent and teacher representatives as a result of the 1980 Education Act.

In 1986 the Government took the process one step further in another Education Act, and from the summer of 1988 all schools were required to elect an increased number of parent-governors for a four-year, rather than the previous two-year, term of office. The situation now stands like this:

Composition of Governing Bodies – 1986 (No.2.) Education Act –

COUNTY AND VOLUNTARY CONTROLLED SCHOOLS

Up to 99 Pupils
2 parents
2 LEA nominees
1 teacher
3 co-opted members
    (or 1 co-opted and
    2 foundation governors
    at controlled schools)
The head-teacher (if s/he
    so chooses)

100-299 Pupils
3 parents
3 LEA nominees
1 teacher
4 co-opted members
    (or 1 co-opted and
    3 foundation)
The head-teacher (if s/he
    so chooses)

300-599 Pupils
4 parents
4 LEA nominees
2 teachers
5 co-opted members
    (or 1 co-opted and
    4 foundation)

600+ Pupils
5 parents
5 LEA nominees
2 teachers
6 co-opted members
    (or 2 co-opted and
    4 foundation)

The head-teacher (if s/he
  so chooses)

The head-teacher (if s/he
  so chooses)

VOLUNTARY AIDED AND SPECIAL AGREEMENT SCHOOLS
(i.e. mainly denominational schools)

Non-foundation governors:

1 parent (at least)
1 LEA nominees (at least)
1 teacher (in schools under 300 pupils)
2 teachers (at least in schools with more than 299 pupils)
1 nominee of a minor Local Authority at primary schools
   serving areas with a minor Authority
The head-teacher (if s/he so chooses)

Foundation governors (one of whom must be a parent) must outnumber the rest by two if the governing body has eighteen or fewer members and by three if it is larger.

Some 100,000 parent-governors are now in office in England and Wales, all of them labouring to come to terms with the consequences of the latest and largest piece of educational legislation, the 1988 Education Reform Act, which will be fully implemented over a period of almost a decade.

WHAT DO GOVERNORS DO?
1. They are responsible for the general conduct of the school.
2. As the various sections of the 1988 Act are introduced, governors must ensure that the school curriculum is broad and balanced, and meets the requirements of the National Curriculum; that courses leading to public examinations are for approved qualifications and follow approved syllabuses; that

the law on collective worship and religious education is complied with; and that information on the curriculum and pupils' achievement are communicated to parents.
3. They must decide whether sex education should be provided at the school and, if so, advise on appropriate content.
4. They can offer the head-teacher general principles to follow in deciding the school's disciplinary policy.
5. They may take part in selecting and appointing school staff, including the head-teacher.
6. They must make statutory information about the school available to parents.
7. They are responsible for preparing an annual report to parents and for holding an annual meeting for parents to discuss the report and any other matters concerning the running of the school.
8. Initially in secondary schools, but later in all schools, they will exercise some rights over the number of children admitted to the school. As a result of the 1988 Act, school admission limits are set at the physical capacity of the school: if the school no longer has space to admit its 'standard number' of pupils (i.e. the number admitted in 1979 or 1989, if that is a larger number) the Local Authority can ask the Secretary of State to agree to a lower number; if, on the other hand, the governors believe there is room to admit more than the official number they may appeal to the Secretary of State if the Local Authority does not agree to this.
9. Many governing bodies already have responsibility for some part of the school's budget. As a result of the 1988 Act, governing bodies of all secondary schools and primary schools with more than 200 pupils will be given greater financial responsibility for managing the whole school budget, for deciding on staffing levels and on recruitment and promotion of teachers.

10. The governors of secondary schools and primary schools with more than 300 pupils will be able to consider whether to apply for grant-maintained status – exchanging Local Authority control for direct funding from the Department of Education and Science. The decision on whether to seek 'opt out' status will be taken by a ballot of parents and rests ultimately with the Secretary of State.

HAVE THE POLITICIANS LOST CONTROL?

In theory the answer to this question should be yes. That is what the Taylor Committee and the Conservative Government, in framing the 1986 Act, intended. Power was to pass from Local Authority nominees to parents, community representatives and teachers. In practice some local politicians of both the major political parties have shown themselves determined to retain as much power as possible in school government. Most Local Education Authorities have always appointed their school governors in proportion to the political strength of the parties on the council: in other words, a council split 70 per cent to Labour and 30 per cent to the Conservatives would appoint political nominees (who need not be councillors but simply interested persons known to support the party concerned) in the ratio 7 to 3. A council split three ways between Conservative, Labour and SLD would split the nominations in the same ratio. Only a few councils have ever tried to reserve all governorships to the majority party alone, and where that has been attempted it has generally met with deep resentment, and been overturned.

The new regulations laid down that the governing bodies which took office in the autumn of 1988 consisted of a majority of parent and teacher representatives and a minority of political nominees. They received recommendations on possible co-opted members from their predecessors as governors – but were under no obligation to approve them. The only advice on co-options from the DES suggested that they should include representatives of local industry and commerce. Given that the political nominees are unlikely to represent one party, and that the parents and teacher representatives together can in any case out-vote the 'politicos' on co-options, it seems very unlikely that any school governing body in future could have an in-built majority support-ing any single political party. But where a single party take all the Local Authority places on a governing body, and are canny in their nomination of co-opted members, perhaps taking the opportunity to infiltrate a few sympathetic supporters that way too, then it is at least in theory possible for control to remain in the hands of one party. The 'politicos' could be out-voted on co-options – but the parents and teachers would have to have their wits about them to ensure they were not hi-jacked at the very first governors' meeting under the terms of the new Act.

HOW TO BECOME A PARENT-GOVERNOR

Parent-governors elected under the terms of the 1986 Act took office in 1988, and are entitled to serve a full term of four years even if their children leave the school during that period. Some may not wish to do so and vacancies caused by resignations will be filled at by-elections, so there will be regular opportunities in many schools for parents to stand for election for the first time. To be eligible to stand, naturally you have to have a child in the school at the time of the election.

The election of governors has to be conducted by a secret ballot. The organization of elections is left to Local Authorities and in some cases the LEA leaves the administration to the individual school. Some arrange a meeting of the parent-teacher association at which candidates can address parents before the vote. Others circulate brief 'manifestos' from each candidate before ballot papers are issued. A row in Kent, where the Local Authority attempted to restrict candidates to a fifty-word biographical statement, was decided in the High Court. To ensure secrecy, ballot papers should be returned in sealed envelopes. The National Association of Governors and Managers issues guidance on how a ballot should be conducted and on who is eligible to vote. In families where natural parents are separated, divorced or re-married, there may be the possibility of dispute over which parents, step-parents or guardians are entitled to vote. Local Authorities may also issue guidance on these issues.

Do you have to be an expert to be a governor? Some schools have reacted to their new responsibilities under the 1988 Education Act by jumping to the conclusion that they will need 'expert' governors in future: the local bank manager to help with the budget, for instance, or an architect or builder to assist in planning school maintenance. Joan Sallis, chairperson of the National Campaign for the Advancement of State Education, regards this as something of an insult to 'ordinary' governors. It is the very ordinariness of parents and community members which is needed, she argues, to help the professionals run schools. If 'experts' are needed they can be brought in to help with specific projects, but no one who is a parent should feel inhibited from standing as a governor because they feel unqualified, she says. Their qualifications are their children and their interest in, and willingness to help, the school they attend.

GOVERNORS' MEETINGS

By law there has to be one meeting of school governors each term, although many boards of governors meet

74

more often than that as the pressure of work increases. At the first meeting of the school year, the governors must elect a chairperson and deputy. All governors, except the teacher representatives, are eligible to stand for these posts, including co-opted members, so the elections must take place after the co-options, and co-opted members must attend the first formal meeting of the board.

The board must also have a clerk, who is responsible for circulating the agenda and reports, taking and circulating the minutes, and for correspondence. In some areas clerks are provided by the Local Authority from amongst their staff, but in others governors have to elect a clerk from their own number, or ask for a volunteer from the teaching staff of the school. Meetings of governors of all schools can be attended by a Local Authority officer.

Meetings of governors follow the usual procedure for committee meetings: an agenda must be circulated at least seven days beforehand. In practice, the agenda is usually drawn up by the head and clerk, but any member may ask for an item to be included; minutes must be kept and attendance recorded. The head-teacher, if not a governor, may attend meetings, and governors may decide who else may be admitted for all or part of the business. Resolutions must be decided by a majority vote, with the chairperson having a casting or second vote in the event of a tie. The agenda and minutes of governors' meetings must be made available for inspection at the school by anyone wishing to see them, and by the LEA. The published minutes may exclude confidential items, which are usually interpreted as items concerning named individual members of staff or named pupils.

COMMITTEES

In some large schools the work of governors has now become so complicated that the boards have set up small sub-committees to handle some of the detailed work. With the advent of financial management in individual schools this may become common practice.

A typical secondary school might find it necessary to set up sub-committees to handle some of the following matters: finance and budgeting, staffing, the curriculum, and buildings and maintenance. The committees would not normally be able to take decisions in their own right, but would prepare detailed reports and recommendations for the main governing body to consider. Final decisions would be made at the regular meetings of the full governing body.

THE ANNUAL MEETING

One of the innovations introduced by the 1986 Education Act was a meeting for parents to consider an annual report from the governors. For governors this was an entirely new departure and was initially not wildly successful in some schools. The drawing up of the annual report – following a formula laid down by the Department of Education and Science – often proved difficult (some were reputedly concocted by the head and the chair of governors without consultation) and some of the parents' meetings called to discuss it proved disastrously ill-attended, or in a few cases not attended by parents at all. A substantial number of schools reported that there were fewer parents present than governors at their first statutory meeting, and teachers were sometimes hostile, and often suspicious of the new proceedings. The signs are, though, that attendances are beginning to improve as parents realize that this is an opportunity to ask questions about the running of the school.

The annual report has to include specific items: the date, time and place of the parents' meeting; the information that the meeting will discuss the governors' 'discharge of their functions'; an account of what consideration has been given to any resolutions passed at the previous meeting (the meeting must have a quorum of 20 per cent of the school's parents in order to be able to pass resolutions); details of who the governors are and where the chairperson and clerk can be contacted; the arrangements for the next parent-governors elections; a financial statement; public examination results; the steps taken to strengthen relations with the community, including the police; and any information about syllabuses and other educational provisions which may have been required by the Secretary of State for Education.

It sounds a dry list, and small wonder that many parents receiving a report which stuck to the letter of what is required proved reluctant to spend their leisure time at a meeting to discuss it. More imaginative schools, though, even for the very first parents' meeting in 1987, used the formula simply as a framework upon which to build a much fuller description of what the school had been doing over the last twelve months. That sort of imaginative report seems to be what brings about a lively meeting which will pull in the punters.

REPORTING BACK TO PARENTS

Parent-governors are elected by parents and many feel an understandable obligation to report back to their electorate rather more fully than through the minutes of governors' meetings, which, of course, parents can read if they wish. Different parent-governors have organized reporting back in various ways. The most common seems to be for parent-governors to attend Parent-Teacher Association meetings regularly and give a personal summary of what the governors have been doing. Obviously they cannot comment on the governors' confidential agenda.

In some schools, parent-governors make sure that they are always represented at meetings and social events, so that they can keep in touch with parental concerns and opinions. And there are schools where parent-governors as well as teachers hold 'surgeries' where parents can approach them for help or advice. Most parent-governors regard themselves as a channel through which individual problems can be taken to the head-teacher and more general parental worries be presented to the governing body, if they are sufficiently serious.

TRAINING FOR GOVERNORS

Most Local Education Authorities provide their governors with some guidance – usually in the form of a booklet – about their duties and responsibilities. Most governors feel the need for more formal training to help them to cope with their increasing responsibilities. When Local Authorities were surveyed in 1987, more than three-quarters of them said that they felt that their current level of governor training was inadequate. This was before the sharp increase in the number of parent and community governors elected and co-opted as a result of the 1986 Act. The Government has invested in governor training through the Education Support Grant system since the 1988 Education Act, and it is expected that this money will be used to build on the foundations already laid by the Local Authorities, colleges and universities, the Open University and the National Association of Governors and Managers, all of whom are involved in producing training materials for governors and in organizing or advising on courses. Governor training is co-ordinated through the Coventry based

Action for Governors' Information and Training to which some Local Authorities are affiliated.

GOVERNORS' RESPONSIBILITIES

Recent legislation gives school governors much greater control over the financial management of their schools, but less over what is taught. So far as the curriculum is concerned, governors have an over-riding duty to ensure that the requirements of the new National Curriculum, and the national testing system which accompanies it, are met. This will be a gradual process, already started in primary schools in the late 1980s, with a timetable running well into the 1990s for the whole ten-subject curriculum, and the four-stage testing procedures at seven, eleven, fourteen and sixteen, to be completely implemented.

Five-year-olds started work on nationally defined English, maths and science in the autumn term of 1989. Eleven-year-olds entering their first year of secondary education started National Curriculum maths and science syllabuses at the same time. One year later, in Autumn 1990, eleven-year-olds are due to start NC English, and eight-year-olds to be launched on NC English, maths and science. In 1991 the first national assessment of seven-year-olds will be carried out on a pilot basis: the following year the first results will be available for parents of seven-year-olds, and the first testing of fourteen-year-olds will begin.

Tests for eleven-year-olds, and for sixteen-year-olds in the subjects in which they are not taking GCSE will follow. So will programmes of study for all the age groups in the three core subjects of English, maths and science, and, in rather less detail, for the further seven foundation subjects of geography, history, art, music, technology, PE, a modern foreign language, and, in Wales, Welsh.

It is clear that for the next six to ten years both primary and secondary schools in England and Wales are going to be involved in a process of rapid change as the new programmes of study and testing procedures are integrated into the lives of teachers and pupils in the schools. Governors, with oversight of the curriculum and a general responsibility for the smooth running of schools, will be closely involved in these changes.

Just a few of the questions they may have to resolve as the 1988 Education Act is implemented are:

(a) Is there sufficient in-service training available to enable teachers to carry out the reform programme in the time available?

(b) Will there be enough replacement staff available to cover for teachers absent on training courses?

(c) Are there enough specialist staff available to the school to allow it to introduce an expansion of science, techology and modern language teaching?

(d) Does the school have sufficient specialist accommodation and equipment to allow it to expand teaching in the directions the Act demands, now or in the foreseeable future?

(e) What are the governors' responsibilities if sufficent staff or accommodation cannot be found to meet the National Curriculum requirements?

(f) Will some teachers be made redundant by the demands of the National Curriculum because their expertise is no longer required?

(g) What are the financial implications for the school of the testing and assessment procedures?

(h) Will there be enough replacement staff available to cover for teachers absent for moderation meetings involved in the testing procedures?

(i) Is the school meeting the requirement for a 'mainly Christian' emphasis in its religious instruction and assemblies?

(j) Does the school have a sufficiently large religious minority amongst its pupils to allow it to apply to hold separate religious assemblies for one or more minority faiths?

LOCAL MANAGEMENT OF SCHOOLS

The answers to all these questions will be influenced by the other major change affecting most schools brought in by the 1988 Education Act, the delegation of the control of school budgets from the Local Authority to individual schools.

There are two distinct parts to the LMS proposals: the establishing of a formula under which all schools in a Local Authority area will be funded, and the delegation of financial control, which will apply to all secondary schools and primary schools with more than 200 pupils – although some Local Authorities have chosen to delegate to their smaller primary schools as well.

FORMULA FUNDING

The Government has laid down very precisely how the new formula by which schools are to be funded is to be worked out: the Local Authority will first assess its total spending on its schools, and deduct from that sum the cost of certain central overheads, for instance the local inspectorate, transport, capital expenditure and central administration and, optionally, a range of other services from school meals to libraries. What remains will be allocated directly to the schools on the basis of a formula drawn up by the Local Authority and approved by the Government. At least 75 per cent of the allocation will be on the basis of the number and ages of the pupils in the school, older pupils bringing in more funds. The other 25 per cent will be allocated on the basis of schools' specific needs, e.g. the provision of an adequate curriculum in small schools, the special educational needs of pupils – these two considerations are compulsory – social deprivation, variations in salary costs in small schools, and variations in premises.

A four-year transitional period will allow schools to adjust to any change between historic and formula funding. Schools will be able to retain any savings and income which accrue to them.

The long-term effect of formula funding is uncertain, but in areas which have experimented with similar schemes there has generally been a shift in funding away from small schools towards the larger. The effect on an individual school will therefore depend to what extent it turns out to be a gainer or a loser under the new formula.

FINANCIAL DELEGATION

The second part of the 1988 Act's financial package involves head-teachers and governors becoming responsible for the day-to-day running of their school's financial affairs. This will inevitably mean a heavier administrative burden within the school, to be carried by the head and other professional and clerical staff under the supervision of the governing body. Information technology packages are being developed and the hardware provided in many areas to ease the load, but the National Association of Head-teachers argues that most secondary schools and some of the larger primary schools will need to employ a bursar or additional administrative assistant when local management is implemented.

The positive side of the reform is that schools will have a new freedom to use their budget in any way they think fit: they will be able to decide on staffing policy, take tenders for minor repair and building work, and 'vire' or transfer money from one budget heading to another as they see fit. They will also be able to keep any income they receive, without affecting their Local Authority grant.

Local management of schools will be phased in by 1994, although schools badly affected by the formula may be allowed a longer transition.

GRANT-MAINTAINED SCHOOLS

Although the decision whether a school should apply for grant-maintained status, opting out of Local Authority control in favour of direct funding from Whitehall, lies in the hands of parents, governors too play a crucial role in the process.

An application for grant-maintained status can be made by any secondary school or a primary school with more than 300 pupils. The procedure can be initiated by the governors, who must endorse it at two consecutive meetings held at least 28 days and not more than 48 days apart. Alternatively the governors must initiate the process if they are requested to do so by a petition of parents numbering at least 20 per cent of the school roll.

The governors must then organize a ballot of all parents at the school, and they are responsible for making sure that all parents understand the issues involved. It is also up to the governors to decide who is eligible to vote in cases of dispute because of divorce, etc. If 50 per cent or more of parents vote in the first ballot, then that decision is binding with a simple majority of those voting. If less than 50 per cent vote, then a second ballot must be held within two weeks and that result is binding whatever the size of the turnout.

Once a decision to apply to opt out is taken by ballot, the governors are responsible for drawing up the detailed proposals which must go to the Secretary of

State for approval.

Once a ballot has been positively concluded, the governors must apply for grant-maintained status within six months. They must issue public notices about the nature of the proposed new school, and provide the Secretary of State with a detailed proposal. If the school is one which is included in a Local Authority reorganization scheme – in other words, if it is faced with closure, amalgamation or a significant change of character such as the loss of its sixth form – then the Secretary of State will consider its application for grant-maintained status before giving his decision on the Local Authority proposals.

The initial governing body of a grant-maintained school will consist of five parents, one or two teachers, the head, and enough 'first' governors to have a majority over the rest. The 'first' governors will be co-opted by the rest in county schools and be appointed by the trustees in voluntary schools. Two of the 'first' governors must be parents when they are appointed and they will serve between five and seven years, longer than the rest of the governing body who will serve the normal four-year term of office.

Once a grant-maintained school is established the governors will have total control of their own budget: they will be able to buy and sell school property, accept gifts, invest money, and enter into contracts with employees. Capital expenditure on the school will now come direct from the DES, not from the Local Authority.

There are, however, restrictions on the extent to which governors may change the character of a grant-maintained school, either by altering its admissions policy or by changing its character or size. These steps can only be taken after five years through statutory procedures leading to an application to the Secretary of State.

GOVERNORS AND THE CURRICULUM

The 1986 Education Act placed upon Local Authorities the duty to provide schools with a policy statement on the curriculum, and gave governing bodies the duty of deciding, in consultation with the head, how that document should be modified for their particular school. Governors must make – and keep up-to-date – a written statement of their conclusions and a copy of this statement must be given to the Local Authority and to the head.

In drawing up their curriculum statement, the governors are not expected to throw the Local Authority document out of the window, according to the DES. They must take professional advice, and also take into account any representation made to them on the curriculum by the local community and by the police.

And there are specific points which the governors must take into account.

CONTROVERSIAL ISSUES

Under Sections 44 and 45 of the 1986 Act, they must forbid the pursuit of partisan political activities by pupils or staff at the school, and where political issues are brought to the attention of pupils, they are to ensure that they are offered a balanced presentation of opposing views.

This does not mean that political issues cannot be taught in schools: but that care must be exercised to deal fairly with controversial issues in class. The DES Circular expanding on this section of the 1986 Act advises that one of the principal functions of education is to prepare pupils for the active discharge of the responsibilities of citizenship. Issues of a controversial political nature will naturally figure in some parts of the curriculum and may arise spontaneously in others. In such cases pupils must be protected from political indoctrination and biased teaching.

According to the DES: 'Sections 44 and 45 should not inhibit schools from dealing with controversial issues within the curriculum. Schools play an essential role in developing and teaching the attitudes, knowledge and skills which are necessary for the proper appreciation of society's fundamental values, notably, its commitment to parliamentary democracy, the freedom of the individual within the law, and the equality of all citizens under the law.

'Among the attitudes, knowledge and skills to be developed are:

(a) A rational and analytical approach to evidence and argument both in forming opinion and resolving differences.
(b) An awareness of the duties and rights of citizenship.
(c) Respect for the law and for the rights of others, including the right to hold their own opinions and to express them within the law.
(d) An understanding of how the law is properly changed and developed.'

To some extent this is an over-simplification of the difficulties schools face in dealing with controversial topics: just what are the 'fundamental values' of a multi-cultural, multi-faith, multi-political society? Does a fair and unbiased discussion of the problems of Northern Ireland have to include views which can no longer be expressed by a legal political party on television? Fundamental values change over time – as they have done on the acceptability of slavery, colonialism, votes for women and race discrimination in Britain and elsewhere – so how can a consensus on fundamental values in the 1980s or 1990s be arrived at by a board of school governors?

SEX EDUCATION

School governors now have the right to decide on whether sex education should be included in the curriculum at all – although the strong advice from the Department of Education and Science is that it should – and what it should consist of if it is to be taught. The 1986 Act lays down that where it is taught it should 'encourage pupils to have due regard to moral considerations and the value of family life'. There is no statutory right for parents to withdraw children from sex education but governors do have the discretion to allow parents to withdraw children if they so request.

Most surveys of parents indicate that the vast majority do want sex education taught throughout the years of schooling in a way that is appropriate to the age of the child. Simple questions about sex and reproduction can arise in the nursery school, and cannot be ignored. Many parents admit to being too shy or embarrassed to tackle the topic at home, and rely on children receiving accurate information at school. The Government has invested money in education about AIDS on the assumption that this will be used as part of sex education courses in secondary schools. Her Majesty's Inspectors recommend that discussion of AIDS should take place separately from the discussion of promiscuity, whether heterosexual or homosexual. And that both the moral and medical aspects of the disease should be addressed.

A discussion of homosexuality is an essential part of any programme of sex education for adolescent children whose sexual preferences will very soon be becoming apparent. Section 28 of the Local Government Act 1988, which bans the 'promotion' of homosexuality by public authorities, is not being interpreted as having any implications for schools, where sex education is under the sole control of the governors. A Circular from the Department of the Environment on the interpretation of

Section 28 states that it will not prevent objective discussion of homosexuality in the classroom, nor the counselling of pupils concerned about their own sexuality.

GOVERNORS AND THE NATIONAL CURRICULUM

Although school governors were given new powers to draw up their school's curriculum policy by the 1986 Education Act, and were specifically asked to take account of community and parental concerns in drawing up that policy, those new powers have been considerably circumscribed by the introduction of a National Curriculum by the 1988 Education Act. This means that through programmes of study, and the regular testing procedures, which will be introduced for the ten compulsory subjects (plus Welsh in Wales) over the next few years, the school curriculum will be largely determined by the National Curriculum Council and the Secretary of State in London. There will be no scope for governors to vary the National Curriculum, and very little school time, especially in the later years of secondary education, to include anything else in the timetable. This will undoubtedly lead to difficulties in schools which wish to keep courses of careers education, personal, social and health education, and social studies on the timetable for all pupils, and threatens some individual subjects such as classics, minority modern languages such as German and Spanish, drama and economics. The introduction of the National Curriculum will take several years, but will bring with it many headaches for conscientious governors who wish to prevent what they see as desirable elements of the curriculum being squeezed out.

GOVERNORS AND THE APPOINTMENT OF STAFF

It is normal practice to include governors on the interviewing panels for senior members of school staff and in particular for the panel appointing a head-teacher. Appointments have to be made according to the rules laid down in the Articles of Government for schools drawn up by the Local Authority. These will vary slightly from one Authority to another, but have the force of law, so the procedures must not be varied. The Local Authority is the actual employer of school staff, except in some voluntary aided schools at present and in grant-maintained schools in future.

Boards of governors often appoint a panel of their members to take charge of appointments, frequently consisting of the head-teacher, the chair of governors, and one or two other members. Membership may be rotated so that all governors take a turn at interviewing, or governors may be invited to offer their services to the panel if the appointment is of particular interest to them or they can offer the panel some special expertise – for instance in languages if a language teacher is being interviewed. It is not usual for the entire board to interview candidates, even for the post of head-teacher, as it can be very intimidating for candidates to face a very large interviewing panel.

Governors should be aware that when interviewing staff there are some questions which may not be asked in the light of equal opportunities and employment legislation. It is not permissible to ask candidates about their marital status or sexual orientation, ethnic origin, religious, trades union or political affiliations, or how the candidate would organize home responsibilities if appointed. Any of these questions could be regarded as prejudicial or discriminatory if taken to a court or tribunal.

WHERE TO FIND OUT MORE
The National Association of Governors and Managers exists to offer advice and support to parent-governors,

and is closely involved in the expanding provision of training for governors. Further information about the work of NAGM, and its publications for governors, can be obtained from the Hon. Secretary, Mrs. Barbara Bullivant, 81 Rustlings Road, Sheffield S11 7AB.

The Advisory Centre for Education also publishes a range of books and pamphlets specifically for governors. Their list of publications is available from ACE Ltd., 118 Victoria Park, London E2 9PB.

6

INFORMATION ABOUT SCHOOLS

Ever since the 1980 Education Act parents have been entitled by law to a substantial amount of information about schools. Their rights have been extended by the new 1988 Act, although it may be well into the 1990s before all the requirements of that Act are being fully met. This section summarizes what parents can expect to be available either from the Local Authority or from schools themselves in the maintained sector.

ADMISSIONS

Every Local Authority must, each school year, publish:

(a) The arrangements for admission of pupils (except to aided or special agreement schools).
(b) The arrangements for educating children in other schools, e.g. in another Local Authority area. (This section should include details on how parents are expected to indicate their preferred school and how they can appeal against a school admission decision.)

Governors of aided or special agreement schools must, each school year, publish:

(a) Their arrangements for the admission of pupils.
(b) Arrangements for appeals against admission decisions.

It is intended that under the 1988 Act grant-maintained schools and City Technology Colleges shall be covered by similar requirements.

The above details must include the number of pupils it is intended to admit to each school in each age-group to which admissions are being made (i.e. some secondary schools admit at eleven and thirteen, for instance); the powers of the Local Authority and the school governors in relation to admissions (heads and governors of aided and controlled schools retain some rights over admissions); the policy followed in deciding on admissions (i.e. the criteria to be used, for instance, by a grammar school or a church-aided school, the weight given to family connections with the school, geographical factors, etc.); the arrangements to be made for pupils living outside the Local Authority's area; and details of any standing arrangements, names of schools, number of places available, etc., in other schools available to pupils but not maintained by the Local Authority.

LOCAL AUTHORITY POLICY

The Local Authority or governors must also publish details of their policy for primary and secondary education. The DES suggests that this should include:

(a) Addresses and telephone numbers of the Authority's headquarters and divisional offices, if any.
(b) A list of maintained primary and secondary schools, including names, addresses, telephone numbers, numbers of pupils, status and character of each school.
(c) The arrangements for transfer between schools at times other than the normal admission points, and the policy followed in arranging transfers.
(d) The arrangements for school transport or assistance with the cost of transport to school.
(e) The arrangements for the provision of free school meals.

(f) Details of policy on the provision of school clothing, or uniform grants, PE kit, etc.

(g) Details of policy on the provision of educational maintenance grants for school pupils.

(h) Policy on entries for public examinations.

(i) The availability of information about the Authority's policy and arrangements for children with special educational needs, their assessment and treatment; the provision which is made for such children in maintained, voluntary and special schools, and in non-maintained or independent special schools.

INFORMATION ABOUT INDIVIDUAL SCHOOLS

The Local Authority or governors, each school year, must publish:

(a) The name, address and telephone number of the school, the number on the roll, status and character and the name of the head-teacher.

(b) The arrangements made for parents who are considering sending their children to the school to visit (i.e. at open days or evenings, through personal interviews with the head or staff, etc).

(c) The range and level of curriculum provided for pupils of different ages and for those with special needs; subject options and choices available, and the arrangements made to consult parents about such choices; the provision made for religious education and the arrangements made for parents to exercise their right of withdrawal from RE; the ways in which sex education is provided; and the provision made for careers education and guidance.

(d) For secondary schools, including special schools with pupils of secondary age:

i) The numbers of pupils each achieving different numbers of passes at A Level and, at GCSE, higher grade passes and all grade passes.

ii) The numbers of pupils awarded each available grade in each subject at A Level and GCSE.

The information above must relate to those age-groups in which the examinations are most commonly taken (i.e. fifth year, seventh year) and must be accompanied by the numbers of pupils in those age-groups. The information under (d(i)) above also has to be published for two successive years afterwards. It is for the Local Authority to ensure that the publication of examination results by schools should be in a common form, by discussion with the governors in the case of aided schools.

(e) The present teaching organization of the school, including arrangements made to teach children of different abilities and ages, and the school's policy on homework.

(f) The arrangements made for pastoral care and discipline and the availability of school rules (corporal punishment, which was included in this section, is now illegal in maintained schools).

(g) The present range of extra-curricular activities provided.

(h) The school's policy on dress, school uniform and its approximate cost.

(i) Any changes in Local Authority policy (i.e. reorganization plans) or proposals by the governors or the head which might change any of the above particulars in future years.

The DES suggests that this information should be published not less than six weeks before the date on which parents are expected to state a preference for a school, and that it should be available in the LEA offices, libraries, and in individual schools for reference and for parents to take away on request. The information should be free, should be kept up-to-date, and Local Authorities and schools should consider whether there is a need to provide it in languages other than English.

In fact most schools now provide most of this information – and many of them much more – in the brochure or prospectus which they publish annually. The 1988 Education Act made the publication of a prospectus obligatory, and governors are required to up-date the information in it as part of their annual report to parents.

INFORMATION ON THE SCHOOL CURRICULUM

The 1988 Act extended the amount of information which must be available to parents on the school curriculum. In future schools will be expected to publish the following:

1. For county and controlled schools, a summary of the governing body's statement of curriculum aims.
2. For a voluntary aided or special agreement school, a summary of the governing body's statement of curriculum aims or, where none such exists, a statement to that effect.
3. A summary of the content and organizations of sex education, and details of how to see any statement of policy on this aspect of the curriculum.
4. The time spent on teaching during each normal school day.
5. The dates of school terms and half-terms for the next school year.
6. A summary for each year group indicating how the curriculum is organized and what it contains, including in particular how the National Curriculum subjects and religious education are organized, what other subjects and cross-curricular themes are included for all pupils and what optional subjects are available and how choices amongst them are constrained.
7. A list of the approved external qualifications for which courses of study are provided.

8. The names of the syllabuses associated with the qualifications above.
9. A list of the external qualifications and names of associated syllabuses offered to those beyond school age.
10. Details of any careers education provided and the arrangements made for work experience.
11. Information about how to make a complaint under Section 23 of the 1988 Act.
12. How to see and, where appropriate acquire, the documents which have to be made available under the 1988 Act (see below).

Governors will be able to decide how to make this information available, and if it is published by the Local Authority, they have no right to alter it in any material way.

PUBLIC ACCESS TO DOCUMENTS

The Regulations, as they are brought into effect, will allow parents and other interested parties access to Local Authority and school documents as follows:

1. For Local Authority maintained schools, the LEA's statement of curriculum policy and, for all maintained schools where it exists, the governors' statement of curriculum aims.
2. All statutory instruments, circulars and administrative memoranda relating to powers and duties under the 1988 Act which are sent to schools by the DES.
3. All published HMI Reports which refer to the school.
4. All schemes of work, widely defined, currently used by teachers in the school.
5. All syllabuses followed, whether for public examinations or not.

6.   For Local Authority maintained schools, a full copy of the arrangements made by the LEA and approved by the Secretary of State for the consideration of complaints about the school curriculum.
7.   In the case of grant-maintained schools, a full copy of the governors' complaints procedure, which must be made under the articles of government.
8.   For all LEA maintained schools, the LEA's agreed syllabus for religious education.
9.   For voluntary schools, a copy of that part of the Trust Deed which governs the provision of religious education and any other written statement which may have been prepared about arrangements for religious education, including any syllabus used in the school.
10. For grant-maintained schools, the religious education arrangements being followed, which will be as under each school's former status.

The Secretary of State has assured schools that sufficient copies of DES documents are provided for schools to meet these requirements. Schools will not be allowed to charge for access to documents, and copies of the school prospectus and the governors' annual report to parents must be provided free. A charge to cover the cost of copying other documents may be made if parents request a personal copy. Some documents which must be available at schools will be covered by Crown Copyright and may not be copied. If available free, they can be obtained from the DES direct, or if a priced publication, from HMSO.

HMI REPORTS ON SCHOOLS

There are approximately 460 HMI in England, with separate inspectorates for Wales and Scotland, whose job is to ensure that standards are maintained in all Local Authority and voluntary schools, colleges and polytechnics. They also have some responsibilities for inspecting university courses and private schools, and they are major producers of reports and statistics on aspects of the education service as a whole and on education policy. From this it is immediately clear that the time they spend in individual schools is very limited. A school may not be visited by an HMI for months or years at a time. Indeed, a full inspection, examining all aspects of a school's work, is a very rare event. In 1987, a group which publishes a regular directory of HMI Reports, concluded that reports take between eleven and eighteen months to issue after an inspection has been made, and that at the present rate of inspecting individual secondary schools, it will take about fifty years for the inspectors to get round them all.

However, inspections of schools do occur, particularly if a school has been reported as having particular problems, and since 1984 the reports on inspections have been published. Under the 1988 Act a school must now make available on request any HMI Report that is available. Private schools are also inspected, and parents considering a private school for a child would be well advised to consult the directory of HMI Reports to see if one is available on any institutions they are considering.

The first thing to notice about an HMI Report, therefore, is the date on which the school was inspected. One of the reasons for reporting at all on schools is to enable them and their governors and the Local Authority to recognize weaknesses and take action to put them right. If a report has been on the shelf a long time, it is reasonable to use it as a basis for asking what action has been taken to improve what the HMI found to be inadequate or unsatisfactory at the time of their visit. The most crucial event to affect a school's performance is undoubtedly the appointment of a new head, so that is something to bear in mind. But other staff changes might be almost as influential in improving a school which had a bad HMI Report some time ago.

There are some other points to note when looking at even up-to-date HMI Reports. Although some are scathing about what the HMI found on their visits and no punches are pulled in complaining about matters as diverse as teaching quality and the quality of the lavatories, most turn out to be much like the curate's egg, good and bad in parts. It is important to note just what the HMI are reporting on – less than half of reports cover all aspects of a school's work – and what has been left out. And while it is the harsher criticisms which may have hit the headlines in the local Press, it is no means unusual to find HMI complimenting other aspects of a school's performance in a report which has had hard things to say about something else.

INTERPRETING EXAMINATION AND ASSESSMENT RESULTS

It is already obligatory for schools to publish their examination results for A Level and GCSE (see above). As the National Curriculum assessment procedure is introduced from the Autumn of 1989, parents will also be provided with additional information about their own child's performance, and their school's performance, in the national assessments which will be introduced for seven-year-olds, eleven-year-olds, fourteen-year-olds and sixteen-year-olds, between 1991 and 1996.

The new system of national assessment is based on ten levels of attainment through which children will be expected to progress from the ages of five to sixteen. Children just starting school might be expected to reach Level 1 in their first year. At seven, when the first assessment will be reported to parents, a child of average ability will reach Level 2. A slow learner might still be on

Level 1, a fast learner at Level 3. And so on up the attainment scale, with an average eleven-year-old being expected to have reached Level 4, an average fourteen-year-old to be on Level 5 or 6, and the top levels coinciding with GCSE grades for sixteen-year-olds. Assessment will be based on a series of targets which will often be assessed in class in the normal course of the day's work by a child's own teacher. More formal tests will be included in the later stages, but some targets may be reached through several subjects, rather than a single one.

Initially, assessment will be confined to the core subjects of the National Curriculum: maths, English and science. The results for individual children will be confidential between teacher and family, but aggregated results for the class and the school will be passed to the Local Education Authority and the Department of Education and Science.

The difficulty in assessing the value of the new results will be the same as that in assessing A Level and GCSE results at present. A parent looking at an individual child's results will be able to judge whether – and what sort of – progress has been made since the last assessment. If there has been little improvement the assessment should help the school to diagnose problems and suggest solutions.

But aggregated results, just like GCSE, will inevitably be affected by the make-up of the school's catchment area as well as its educational competence.

In other words, a primary school which draws its children from an area with a high proportion of professional families is likely to have more of its five and six-year-olds reading fluently than one with a high proportion of children from relatively deprived homes, or homes where English is not the first language. In the former school, many children may have learned to read before they even started in the reception class.

Secondary schools show the same sort of discrepancy in performance at GCSE and at A Level. The latter results particularly are very much a reflection of the proportion of pupils who have decided voluntarily to stay on after the normal school-leaving age, which again reflects the expectations of families when formal education should ideally end: at sixteen or eighteen or later.

This is not to say that individual schools do not make a difference. All the latest research shows that schools with very similar intakes can produce very different results: that, in effect, good schools can 'add value' to what might be expected of children according to their social background. Even so, this does not necessarily explain all the differences in performance between schools, and the 1988 Education Act requirement for the publication of all assessment results, as and when the tests are introduced over the next few years, allows schools to provide parents with some additional factual information on their intakes and catchment areas. This should be carefully balanced with everything else that is known about a school. What look like brilliant results on paper may actually conceal a school which is failing to help a large proportion of its children fulfil their potential. Poor results may come from a school with a particularly difficult intake where the pupils are being well taught and achieving results well beyond what might have been predicted. Results are not always what they seem.

FINDING OUT ABOUT INDEPENDENT AND OTHER SCHOOLS

Some seven per cent of British children attend fee-paying independent schools, and from 1989 there has also been a category of school – free to the pupil but independent of Local Authority control – which forms a sort of half-way house between the maintained and independent sectors. These are grant-maintained schools, which are former State schools which have opted for direct funding by the Department of Education and Science, and City Technology Colleges. The latter have been funded partly by industry and commerce, although still with a heavy input from the DES, and will be exempted from the provisions of the National Curriculum, having instead a curriculum biased towards science, technology, commerce, and in one case, the performing arts.

Local Authorities should be able to inform parents of the existence of fully independent and GM and CTC schools in their areas. It is then up to parents to obtain a prospectus from any of the schools in which they are particularly interested. Fully independent schools are also listed in some reference books, and comprehensive details are given in the *Independent Schools Year Book* and the *Preparatory Schools Year Book*. The Independent Schools Information Service (see page 216) also provides information to parents and there are private agencies which will advise on the suitability of particular schools, fees and on insurance policies to provide income to pay fees.

None of the statutory requirements on information for parents apply to independent schools, although most publish prospectuses and reputable schools will be willing to answer all, or any, of the questions which parents might ask.

The majority of private secondary schools select by academic ability for entry, as do some prep and pre-prep schools for younger children. Those which select should be expected to publish their examination results, and in many cases these will look understandably more impressive than those for a comprehensive school which admits children of all abilities from its neighbourhood. HMI Reports are rare in the private sector, but some do exist and include comments very critical of individual schools. As mentioned earlier, the DES Index of HMI Reports will indicate whether a report is available for a particular school.

Not all private schools are highly academic. Some have been pioneers in 'progressive' methods of education; some specialize in dealing with children and young people with special needs, or with emotional difficulties, and may be available to parents through their Local Authority without charge; and others specialize in educating children with particular talents in music, art, drama, etc., in which case, again, Local Authorities may be prepared to help with fees for particularly gifted children.

COSTS IN MAINTAINED SCHOOLS

Education in maintained schools has been provided free of charge for all pupils since the 1944 Education Act. However, this has never meant that some charges do not inevitably fall on parents, and that some families do not find these occasionally difficult to meet.

Local Authorities have the right to assist families with some costs. They must provide free school meals for families on income support, but no longer have any discretion to extend this benefit to other children. The free meals must be provided even where the Local Authority no longer offers a school meal service as such, and in this case arrangements are usually made to provide sandwiches at midday to those who qualify for this benefit. Local Authorities can also provide assistance for parents with school clothing, including PE kit, and provide maintenance allowances for pupils staying on at school beyond the official school-leaving age. Whether, and to what extent, this help is available varies from one Local Authority area to another, but LEAs must publish their policy on these matters.

Schools have also generally made some charge for various activities both in and out of school time: for instrumental music lessons, ingredients for cookery classes, materials for crafts and needlework or for travel on school visits, field-trips and longer visits or holidays organized by the school.

The 1988 Education Act legislated on the charging policy in schools in an attempt to clarify the law. In principle, the Act lays down that activities cannot be charged for if they take place 'wholly or mainly' during school hours or if they are essential to the National Curriculum or to an examination course. However, the DES guidance still allows some loopholes: activities might be arranged during school hours, for instance, but children given leave of absence to take part, in which case charging would be allowed. The traditional school ski-ing holiday could come under this heading, and in any case could be legally charged for if the charge were made by a travel agency rather than directly by the school. The question as to what is an essential part of the curriculum – a geography field-trip, a theatre visit to see a GCSE set-play performed? – is also open to wide interpretation. And the encouragement of 'voluntary' contributions can also apparently continue, although children could not be excluded from a visit if their parents refused to pay voluntarily, which in some cases might make a visit so uneconomic to organize that it could not take place at all. Much of this part of the Act may well have to be interpreted by the courts as schools explore what is legal and what is not.

7

CHOOSING A SCHOOL

Since the 1981 Education Act, parents have had some rights to select a maintained school place for their child. These rights have been strengthened by subsequent legislation, particularly the 'open enrolment' provisions of the 1988 Education Act which will come into force in 1990 for secondary schools, and later for primary schools.

So how much choice is there in reality? The answer is, inevitably, only limited choice. If a school is full, the parental right to choose will be of less account than the criteria the Local Authority sets for determining which children shall be accepted and which turned away. Geography too is a powerful restraint on free choice. If there is only one primary school in your village or one secondary school in your town, then it is inevitable that most families will have to accept what is on offer. Only those who are wealthy enough to choose the private sector, or transport their children long distances to an alternative school, will have any meaningful choice at all.

ADMISSIONS ARRANGEMENTS

Local Authorities and maintained schools must now publish their arrangements for admissions to schools, and these will differ according to whether the school is a county school or voluntary aided, i.e. a school, often with a church affiliation, which maintains some financial control over its own buildings and admissions.

In county schools the Local Authority will lay down the admissions policy, and be responsible for its administration. They will, for instance, write to all parents whose children are about to enter primary school, and those about to transfer to middle or secondary schools, outlining the options available. They must publish the criteria they will use to allocate children to a school which is over-subscribed. Priority is generally given to children living nearest to the school, children with brothers and sisters already there, children with specific medical reasons for attending a particular school, etc.

Voluntary aided schools have to agree their admissions policy with the Local Authority but responsibility for carrying it out is delegated to the head and governors. Schools with a church affiliation give preference to families of their particular faith. This is quite legal so long as the criterion is made clear to parents in advance.

Grammar schools are entitled to demand that entrants have passed the Local Authority's selection test or examination at eleven, and may wish to test older applicants moving in from other areas before accepting them. It is not legal for other schools to discriminate against applicants on the grounds of their academic ability.

Grant-maintained schools will be able to set their own criteria for admissions, although these must not take into account a child's ability if the school is comprehensive. The Government seems to accept that a school which becomes grant maintained will continue to take the children from its traditional catchment area, at least initially. A GM school will not be permitted to change its character, i.e. from comprehensive to grammar, or vice versa, for at least five years.

City Technology Colleges, which are being set up in some areas with the help of funding from industry and commerce, are intended to be comprehensive in their intake, but they are permitted to select children on the grounds of their, and their family's, commitment to the technologically-biased education on offer and to education up to the age of eighteen. The early CTCs have interviewed candidates and their parents where demand has outstripped the supply of places.

Private schools set their own criteria for admission. Some form of entrance test or examination is common, even at the junior or infant stage, and senior schools recruiting at eleven or thirteen usually require entrants to have passed the Common Entrance Examination at a specific level. It is common for private schools also to interview applicants, and possibly their parents, before they offer a place. Some private schools have long waiting lists for admission and it is not uncommon for children's names to be put down for the most famous schools at birth. The Assisted Places Scheme provides help with fees for children whose parents wish them to attend private day schools, but whose financial status makes this difficult.

OPEN ENROLMENT

Before the 1988 Education Act, Local Authorities who had a surplus of school places were entitled to spread pupils around by means of planned admission limits. This meant that as the number of children entering school dropped – as it had done consistently since the early 1970s, only now beginning to rise again for the primary age-groups – places might be deliberately left empty at a popular school in order to boost numbers elsewhere. The aim was to keep all the schools which would be needed in the long term running at an economic level while numbers were low.

Needless to say, this was a policy which angered parents who were turned away from the school of their choice. Parents in Dewsbury, in West Yorkshire, made history when they challenged their Local Authority's planned admission limit policy in the courts, kept their children out of school for a year, and eventually won the right to have them attend the school they preferred.

In fact the Kirklees Authority had done nothing illegal. They lost the case on a technicality. But the Dewsbury case was in many ways the last nail in the coffin of a policy which had become extremely unpopular with parents, and was abolished by the 1988 Act. From September 1990 all secondary schools will be required to admit pupils up to the physical capacity of the school. Admissions to primary schools will be made on the same basis at a later date.

The definition of the physical capacity of the school, though, looks like providing another fruitful source of debate between the administrators, parents and school staff. In theory the standard number of pupils who can be admitted will be set according to the number admitted in 1979, or 1989, whichever is the larger. In practice, though, there will be argument about the extent to which the use of school buildings has changed over time, the extent to which temporary classrooms, possibly in poor repair, should be taken into account, and the extent to which children in the late 1980s, studying different syllabuses and often involved in a great deal more practical work than in previous generations, need more space than they had ten years ago. There will undoubtedly be disputes in those primary schools where empty classrooms have been adapted for use as a school library, a parents' room, or even for the use of a nursery class or playgroup. It is not yet clear whether the DES will regard these adapted spaces as potential classrooms if and when demand for places rises.

The Local Authority or the school governors can set an admission limit higher than the school's standard number, but not a lower one. Any dispute between them will ultimately be settled by the Secretary of State for Education. In any case the standard number has to be reviewed regularly in the light of the needs of pupils and the accommodation available, and if the governors or Local Authority feel that a lower figure should be set, then they can apply to the Secretary of State.

APPEALS

If school governors or the Local Authority refuse a child a place at a school, then parents have a right of appeal. The Local Authority's appeal committee may have a majority of Local Authority or governor members, but these members must not take the chair, and the committee may also include one or more parents.

When an application for a school place is turned down, the Local Authority or governors must inform parents of their right to appeal, and how they should set about this. An appeal must be made in writing setting out the reasons for challenging the decision. Parents may appear in person at the appeal hearing, must be given the opportunity to speak, and may, at the discretion of the committee, be accompanied by a friend or representative. The committee's decision, which is binding on the Local Authority or school governing body concerned, must be sent to the parents in writing and include reasons for accepting or rejecting the appeal.

Appeals against school admissions decisions have a good record of success – varying between 30 and 50 per cent in different areas of the country. It is therefore worth appealing, and worth taking considerable trouble to present a child's case as fully as possible.

The initial letter of appeal must state a family's reasons for challenging the admission decision. Reasons which carry weight include: brothers and sisters already attending the school; other family links with the school; the closeness of the school to home – or the inconvenience of the alternative school offered; preference for single sex or co-education; preference for a denominational or non-denominational school; close friends attending the same school; medical or psychological reasons; educational reasons, i.e. curriculum, discipline, etc.; in Wales, a preference for a Welsh or English-language school. It is also reasonable to explain why the family does not want the alternative school being offered.

The Local Authority should give at least fourteen days' notice of the time and place of the appeal hearing, and if it is not possible for the parents (or parent) to attend on that day, for good reason, then the clerk should be informed immediately so that the hearing can be post-poned to another date.

The hearing itself will offer the Authority and the parents a chance to put their case, and question each other, and sum up. Parents should feel free to question anything they do not understand, and challenge any-thing they disagree with.

The committee has the right to suggest that the parents accept a place at a third school – neither their preference nor the alternative offered by the Authority. In that case the hearing should be adjourned to enable the parents to consider this new offer. If it is rejected, they should have the opportunity to argue against it before the committee considers its final decision.

The appeal committee must inform parents in writing of its decision and its reasons. If the appeal is turned down, the parents must then decide whether to accept the school place offered. Further legal action is very limited. The Secretary of State's powers to intervene in admissions cases was reduced by the 1980 Education Act, although there is still the right to appeal to the DES if you think the Local Authority or school governors have acted unreasonably. The chances of success, on past experience, though, are extremely limited. It is also possible to appeal through a local councillor to the

Ombudsman about the composition of the appeal committee or the way that the appeal was conducted. This procedure allows maladministration to be investigated.

HOW TO JUDGE A SCHOOL

This is undoubtedly the most difficult judgement that parents have to make, and even the most knowledgeable and experienced – i.e. parents who are teachers themselves – occasionally get it wrong.

There are several reasons for this. The first is simply that the judgement is inevitably subjective. An institution – even a small school – is made up of a complex and changing series of relationships, and what may suit one child may not necessarily suit another. Even so, it is generally accepted now that schools do vary in their quality and that there are some reasonably objective ways for parents to judge that quality.

Here is a simple check-list of how to set about choosing a short-list of schools in your area – or further afield if you are prepared for your children to board.

1. Get all the information on schools from your Local Authority and the directories of private schools (see previous chapter).
2. Draw up a short-list based on your basic preferences: distance from home, travelling times, single sex or co-educational, day or boarding, State or fee-paying, denominational or non-denominational.
3. Collect all the additional written information listed in the previous chapter about the schools of your choice.
4. Arrange to visit as many of the most likely schools as you can manage. It is vital to visit a school before choosing it: local gossip and even national reputation can be very misleading and is often out-of-date. Schools do change, for better and worse, particularly if there has been a change of head-teacher.

WHAT TO LOOK FOR ON A SCHOOL VISIT

First impressions are not always wrong. It is not so long ago that some maintained schools had notices in the playground effectively warning parents to keep out. Attitudes have changed, but it is still fair to judge whether, as a visiting parent, you are treated courteously by all those you have contact with, whether the school is welcoming and well signposted for visitors, and whether the atmosphere is friendly, orderly and constructive. Is this a place, in other words, where you think your particular child will learn happily for the next several years?

Two important points to make. What worries parents most about schools are the two areas which are hardest to judge, discipline and standards, particularly in secondary schools. In neither case is it always wise to judge simply on what is written down in the school brochure. Lists of school rules and punishments and strict codes for dress do not tell you how children behave in practice. You can judge that for yourself to some extent by visiting the school. Similarly, lists of examination successes at GCSE and A Level may look good, but are the least you might expect at a grammar school or a selective independent school. It is even sensible to be suspicious of a comprehensive school which does not offer many subjects or gain many passes at either examination level, even allowing for the fact that a comprehensive takes the whole ability range, not just the academically most able children in the neighbourhood. But again, the written record may be deceptive. A school which looks creditable on paper may benefit from a high proportion of well-motivated children who are actually not performing as well as they should. A school with few examination successes to its name may be getting the very best out of an intake who come from less supportive homes with no tradition of doing well at school. What matters is the progress children make in school from the base of their achievement when they enter. And that is not as easy to measure as it looks.

It is as well to have a set of questions in mind before embarking on a school visit. Some you will want to put to staff directly. Others you may be able to answer for yourself after looking around the school and seeing staff and children at work. No one can decide for a family what makes a good school for their child: some parents will find some aspects of schooling more important than others. There are differences of opinion, for instance, over co-education, school uniform, and even over whether modern or elderly buildings make a difference to the quality of children's education. But here are some questions, some practical, some more subjective, which may help parents reach a decision.

AT PRIMARY SCHOOL

1. What are the arrangements for children to visit before starting?
2. If four-year-olds are admitted, are there any extra non-teaching staff in their classes, as there would be in a nursery class?
3. How big are the classes, and are they smaller for the youngest children?
4. What are the arrangements for settling children in during their first few weeks?
5. Is any special help given to summer-born children who are often late starters and can fall behind?
6. How are the teaching groups arranged? Not all primary schools teach in year groups, with all the five-year-olds together, and so on. Arrangements should be stable.
7. How long does a single teacher stay with one class? And do the older children work at all with specialist teachers? Continuity is important to young children.

8. Does the school provide parents with details of its curriculum, reading schemes, etc.
9. Are parents expected to work with the teacher in a formal way, reading at home with children, for instance? It helps.
10. Does the school put a high priority on the children's creative as well as academic work? Look at the displays around the school for an answer!
11. How are children prepared for their move to their next school?

AT SECONDARY SCHOOL
1. How are children introduced to the school in the first week or so?
2. Are the younger children treated in any way differently from the older ones: by being taught in separate buildings, for instance, or by playing in a more protected area? Eleven-year-olds can find their new secondary school a bit overwhelming.
3. How is the school organized in terms of classes, teaching groups, houses, sixth-form accommodation, etc?
4. Who is the person mainly responsible for the welfare of the individual child? One person (at least) should know a child well.
5. How does the school report back to parents on progress or if there are problems?
6. How does it make arrangements for particularly slow learners? And for the particularly gifted child?
7. How do the older students treat the younger children? Bullying should not be tolerated.
8. What is the school's policy on homework? It should have one.
9. Is a check made on whether homework is not only done but also marked regularly?

10. What are the arrangements for choice of exam subjects, careers education, and transfer into the sixth form, local colleges or higher education?

AT ALL SCHOOLS

1. How does the school organize its teaching: by ability, age, or in some other sort of group? What is crucial is not the system but the staff's commitment to it.
2. What are the school's rules and sanctions on uniform, discipline, etc. Rewards are more effective than punishments.
3. If teaching is organized in ability groups, how are transfers made for children who are wrongly placed?
4. How large are the classes and/or other teaching groups? Small is generally better, though tiny sixth-form groups may be taking staff away from younger classes.
5. How many teachers are there and how frequently do staff leave? High staff turnover is a bad sign.
6. If the school is co-educational, what does the school do to ensure that boys and girls have equal opportunities to perform well across the whole curriculum?
7. Are there special arrangements to help families whose first language is not English?
8. What is the school's policy to promote good race relations?
9. What arrangements are made to allow parents and staff to discuss progress?
10. What written reports, if any, are made to parents? Annual written reports will soon be compulsory.
11. What does the school do to keep parents in touch if there are problems, and are there any special facilities for pupils in difficulties with work or behaviour?
12. What part do parents play in the everyday life of the school?

13. Is there a PTA, a parents' room, and easy communication with parent-governors?
14. What activities are there for children out of school time?
15. Are there any plans for new buildings, or reorganization which might affect the future of the school?

JUDGING STANDARDS

The hardest thing to judge in any school is the quality of the learning that is going on there. But there are some pointers, and they are backed up by research which tries to identify why some schools perform better than others for children of similar background and ability. The introduction of programmes of study and attainment targets for the National Curriculum will give parents a more objective measure of how well their children are doing once they enter a school, but this does not necessarily help with the initial choice. Here are some points to look for on a visit.

1. Is children's work well presented and displayed around the school?
2. Are their books in good condition and is work well presented in them?
3. Is the work going on in classrooms disciplined and well-ordered, which does not necessarily mean that the pupils will be sitting silently in rows. A great deal of class-work these days involves discussion and practical work, but this should not degenerate into chaos.
4. How well looked after are the school premises? Even old buildings can be kept clean and pleasant. Is there evidence of graffiti on the walls and rubbish in the playgrounds? Are the toilets clean and undamaged?

5. Is the relationship between children and teachers relaxed and friendly or do the teachers seem tense and the children disorderly? Do any of the children look bored, or sulky or cowed?
6. Do staff appear to welcome parents as visitors and show confidence in explaining what they are doing?
7. Can staff explain clearly how they expect children to progress from year to year, and what arrangements they make for children who need special help at one time or another?
8. Is the school well-equipped for practical and creative subjects like design technology, information technology, home economics, business studies, art, music and for science? Primary schools, as well as secondary schools, are expected to teach science and technology under the terms of the National Curriculum. Are computers in evidence and are they being used? Is there an adequate library and is that being used by children?

8

CHANGING SCHOOLS

There are two main reasons why a family might wish to change a child from one school to another. They might be moving home, or they might have become so dissatisfied with a school that they have decided that a change is essential. The reasons for that decision are discussed in Chapter 14. Either way, the change can be disruptive to the child, however beneficial the long-term effects. And in either case the move should be planned as carefully as possible. This chapter will deal with the mechanics of making a change, which in many ways are similar to the mechanics of choosing a school in the first place.

STATING A PREFERENCE

The right of families to state a preference for a particular maintained school apply just as much if a change of school is being negotiated as in the first instance when starting school at one of the normal times. The same information about schools should be available to a family moving into a new Local Authority area as to parents already living there when school choices are made. Similarly, if a school is full in the year-group concerned, the Local Authority may turn down a request for a place, and the family has the normal right to appeal against that decision (see Chapter 7). Most schools, both maintained and private, experience occasional vacancies in all year-groups, however, as pupils leave for a variety of reasons, so there is no reason for being deterred from applying for a place at a popular school which is said to be always full if you are looking for a place for a child in a year-group other than the normal starting one. There may well be a vacancy.

WHEN IS THE BEST TIME?

Families do not always have much choice about when to move a child from one school to another if a move of house is also involved. If the move is a voluntary one, however, or if the distances involved are not great, then it is clearly better to make the move at the beginning of a school year, or the beginning of a term, rather than in the middle.

In particular, it is best not to move a pupil in the middle of an examination course – subject options and examination syllabuses and teaching methods vary widely from one school to another. This will remain true to some extent even after the National Curriculum has been fully introduced. A change half-way through a GCSE or an A Level course can be a severe disadvantage. That is something to be avoided if at all possible, and some families go to the lengths of leaving a child behind with friends or relatives if they are close to examinations when the family has to move house, so that they can complete their course without disruption.

If a child is being moved because of unhappiness at school, then the disruption of a move has to be weighed against the damage staying in the same school may cause. That is a difficult decision which can only be made in the light of all the personalities involved. Unhappy children are unlikely to learn much and it may be that a new start is preferable whatever the disruption involved.

Whatever the reason for moving a child from one school to another, the procedure is essentially the same. It is neither legal nor desirable to keep a child out of school for long, so it is necessary to arrange a place at the new school before withdrawing from the old. Once that is done, in the State sector, it is simply necessary to inform the head that you are withdrawing a child. The head may ask for the name of the new school so that records can be passed on. In a fee-paying school there may be some liability for fees until the end of the term or year. The exact liability should have been made clear when the child was registered as a pupil.

INFORMAL ADVICE ABOUT SCHOOLS

Although families moving to a new area are entitled to all the same information available to parents already there, this is not necessarily as useful to them when they are living at a distance, and have none of the local knowledge and informal contacts with other parents they would have if they had lived in the area for years. It is sometimes possible to gain access to an informal network of information about schools by contacting the local branch of the Campaign for the Advancement of State Education or the local federation of Parent-Teacher Associations. The national offices of both organizations can put you in touch with their local branches, if any.

STATE TO PRIVATE OR VICE VERSA?

An increasing number of parents make use of both the State and the private sectors of education during a child's school career, or use both sectors for different children in the same family. The major cross-over points between the two sectors are at seven or eight, when traditional 'prep school' education starts; at eleven or thirteen, at the beginning of secondary education; and at sixteen, when A Level and other post-sixteen courses begin. In the first case, the switch is more usually from a maintained primary school into a private prep or secondary school. At sixteen there is a steady flow of private school pupils into maintained school sixth forms, or sixth-form or tertiary colleges.

Major factors in making these decisions appear to be

firstly the availability of single-sex secondary education, which has been declining more quickly in the State sector than it has in the private, although many private schools are also switching to co-education; secondly, the availability of boarding facilities, which are not widely available in the maintained sector; smaller classes and better facilities in some (not all) private schools; and lastly, dissatisfaction with maintained schools, mainly on the grounds that they fail to cater adequately for 'bright' children, or for children with particular problems. A high proportion of parents with children in private schools are 'first-time' buyers who themselves attended grammar schools and dislike the comprehensive system.

There does not seem to be any evidence that children find it particularly difficult to switch from one sector to another. The biggest difference most children report is in accent – and children are adept at adjusting their speech patterns so as not to stand out from the crowd for long.

A CHANGE AT SIXTEEN

While parents may be able to impose single sex education on a child at eleven or thirteen , by the age of sixteen many young people make a stand in favour of co-education and seek a change of school on those grounds for their post-sixteen studies. Others have simply became tired of boarding education, or feel the need for a change of school, particularly if they have been in a private school, as is possible, from the age of seven, or even five.

There are two possibilities open to discontented fifth formers. Firstly, a move from a private school to a State sixth form, or vice versa, which may involve also a switch from single sex to co-education. There has been a steady move by the major boys' private schools to recruit girls into their sixth forms and many girls take advantage of this by moving out of all-girls schools into mixed sixth forms within the private as well as the State sectors.

The second possibility is a move into a sixth form or tertiary college, institutions almost exclusively found in the maintained sector, although there are a handful of private sixth-form colleges in the South East of England. A sixth-form college will concentrate on providing mainly academic courses such as A and AS Levels, but in drawing its clientele from a number of feeder schools is likely to be able to provide a much wider range of courses than a school sixth form. A tertiary college takes this process one stage further by bringing together academic and vocational courses (previously provided only in colleges of further education) for students over sixteen, and so offering a wider choice still, including the possibility of taking A Levels and vocational courses in combination. Both types of college have proved success-ful in attracting young people from traditional sixth-form education in private and State schools. The academic record of sixth-form and tertiary colleges is good, and they seem to be particularly successful in pushing up the proportion of young people prepared to stay in education beyond school-leaving age in areas where they have been introduced.

An application to join another institution at sixteen will have to be made to the head or principal early in the academic year, certainly before the end of the Spring term. There may be some academic qualification required for A Level study – good grades in five or six GCSEs, for example – and if the facility is popular locally there may be an admission limit in force at maintained sector schools and colleges. In addition there may be a limit on the number of students accepted for particular courses. Early application is advisable.

9

EDUCATION OUT OF SCHOOL

There are families who decide, for a number of different reasons, to educate their children outside the normal school system. It is often believed that the law on education states that children must go to school. If fact, the law is less specific, and merely lays upon parents the duty of ensuring that children are educated according to their age, aptitude and ability, or their special needs, by attendance at school 'or otherwise'. Those two words have been taken literally by thousands of families who form what is generally known as the Education Otherwise movement. Education Otherwise is also the name of the main advisory and support group which such families have formed and which any parents interested in home education should undoubtedly contact.

There are two main reasons why families decide to educate their children themselves. Some are convinced that they wish to continue the education they have started with their under fives beyond the official school starting age. They want the responsibility for education to remain within the family, and they often feel that children will learn more effectively and on the basis of different values if they stay at home. Such families opt for Education Otherwise as a matter of principle, believing from the beginning that they can do as good a job for their children as the school system can.

Other families seem to turn to Education Otherwise in a state of some disillusionment with the school system as their children have found it. They find that their children – of almost any age – are made unhappy or positively disturbed by the school education they are receiving and feel that they would become happier and be enabled to learn more effectively out of school. Even as early as the first term at primary school, some families find that school is having a bad effect on their children's behaviour and attitudes. Families report that primary children have become bad-tempered, frustrated, aggressive, depressed and thoroughly negative about school. Others feel that schools place too high an emphasis on competition and that this blunts children's natural appetite for and enjoyment of learning.

Education Otherwise is not something to be embarked upon lightly. Although the legal right of parents to educate their own children if they wish is firmly established, Local Authorities have the duty to ensure that the education being provided is appropriate and efficient, and officialdom does not always find it easy to adapt to the non-conformist family in its midst. Education Otherwise also requires from parents – or at least from one parent – a commitment in time and energy which has to be almost total.

As one Education Otherwise parent put it: 'The children have been educated at home for nine months and during that time I feel I have unlearned so much it almost hurts. But it is a healthy sort of strain, like exercising muscles that have been disused since child-hood. I have had days of doubt about whether I can stand to have no peace and quiet ever again, and the odd whim to pursue a career of my own, but I know that I will never be able to hand over the reins of my children's lives to another body unless it is at their request.'

FIRST STEPS

Education Otherwise advises families not to embark on home teaching without a great deal of thought and preparation. It is vital to understand the legal position, and the rights and duties of the Local Authority in relation to children being taught at home. And it is highly advisable to have read all the literature on home teaching and to have discussed the options with families who have already taken a similar step. One of the organization's prime objectives is to bring families educating their children at home into contact with each other for mutual advice and support.

THE LAW

The relevant section of the law is Section 36 of the 1944 Education Act, as amended by the 1981 Education Act. This states:

'It shall be the duty of the parent of every child of compulsory school age to cause him to receive efficient full-time education suitable to his age, aptitude and ability and to any special educational needs he may have, either by regular attendance at school or otherwise.'

This is backed up by Section 76:

'In the exercise and performance of all powers and duties conferred and imposed upon them by this Act the Minister and Local Education Authorities shall have regard to the general principle that, so far as is compatible with the provision of efficient instruction and training and the avoidance of unreasonable public expenditure, pupils are to be educated in accordance with the wishes of their parents.'

However, Local Education Authorities also have duties under the same Act, Section 37 (i):

'If it appears to a Local Education Authority that the parent of any child of compulsory school age in their area is failing to perform the duty imposed on him . . . it shall be the duty of the Local Authority to serve upon the parent a notice requiring him . . . to satisfy the Authority that the child is receiving efficient full-time education suitable to his age, ability and aptitude either by regular attendance at school or otherwise.'

If parents fail to satisfy the Local Authority it may serve a school attendance order on them, and if this is not complied with, it may eventually take them to court, where the ultimate sanction will be the imposition of a care order to ensure that the child is properly educated.

This may sound daunting, but in practice most Education Otherwise families find that once they have explained exactly what they are doing, their LEA is co-operative, and a constructive relationship is worked out between the family and the official – usually an adviser – who is charged with the responsibility of seeing that the parents are fulfilling their educational duty towards their child or children.

REGISTRATION AND DE-REGISTRATION

All schools have to keep admission and attendance registers, but children will not be officially registered until they have actually attended school. Legally this means it is sometimes easier for a family never to send a child to school than to remove one who has already started. However, families have successfully removed children from the system at secondary as well as primary age, so this need not necessarily be any deterrent. In a case where a child is unhappy at school, or refusing to go, de-registration may not only be necessary but urgent.

Parents wishing to de-register a child must inform the head-teacher in writing. In some cases the head or the Local Authority may refuse to de-register the child, and this may lay parents open to legal proceedings if they take the child away anyway. This area of the law does not appear to be very clear, and parents may need to seek legal advice to deal with it.

If a child is not already registered at school there is no obligation to inform the Local Authority that you intend to educate at home. However, families are liable to be visited by either an Educational Welfare Officer or an adviser, and have to produce evidence that they are providing an efficient education. In these circumstances it may be wiser to inform the Local Education Authority of the family's plans early on, so as to gain their support, or at least acquiescence, and pre-empt future problems.

UNJUSTIFIED DEMANDS

According to Education Otherwise, the Local Authority has no legal right to demand any of the following:

(a) That education should be held in a classroom or in any other particular place, or that they should follow a classroom or formal lesson style of learning.

(b) That anyone concerned with the child's education should be a qualified teacher.

(c) That the education offered should follow a similar syllabus to that being offered at school, or should meet any particular standard of school work.

GETTING LEGAL ADVICE

Education Otherwise offers legal advice and support to members, but not legal representation, which may prove necessary if a family finds itself in confrontation with the Local Education Authority. An understanding solicitor can be found either through the National Council for Civil Liberties, a national organization sympathetic to Education Otherwise, or through the Citizens Advice Bureau locally. There is, however, a shortage of lawyers experienced in this area because cases are rare. Legal advice can be expensive and families may not be eligible for legal aid for cases of this kind. Advice on legal aid eligibility can also be obtained from the CAB.

LOCAL AUTHORITY OFFICERS

If a child is removed from school, the first Local Authority official likely to contact a family is the

Education Welfare Officer, whose major responsibility is to enforce school attendance. As a family determined to educate at home is very different from one whose children are playing truant or avoidably absent from school for other reasons, it is sensible to ask the EWO to pass the family's file to an educational adviser who can make some assessment of the educational plans being made for the child or children concerned.

Local Authority advisers (in some areas known as inspectors, but not to be confused with HMI, Her Majesty's Inspectors, who have no local or individual responsibilities) usually specialize either in a single academic subject – maths, English or science – or in a particular stage of education – primary or secondary. Education Otherwise families report that they get particularly useful help from the latter, who can advise across the whole range of primary or secondary subjects.

The majority of families who have embarked upon Education Otherwise report that they have not been harassed or threatened with legal proceedings by their Local Authority, and have often received a great deal of support and encouragement from individual officers.

PART-TIME SCHOOLING

There is no legal obligation upon the Local Authority to provide part-time schooling for families who feel that their children are better off without the full-time variety. However, some head-teachers have been co-operative with Education Otherwise families and have allowed children to attend school for particular activities such as sport, music or chess, or even just for play-time, so that social contact with other local children is maintained.

There are, however, legal difficulties. Parents should check with the head-teacher or Local Authority that children are insured while they are on school premises. And many heads are reluctant to take on 'unofficial' pupils for the very good reason that they receive no financial allowance for them.

RETURNING TO SCHOOL

Many children who have been educated at home for a time have returned successfully to the normal school system, and have performed well academically later in their education. Provided the child actually wants to go to school for the first time, or return after a time away, it should not be much more difficult settling in than if the child was changing school. The biggest change will be the social one: the switch from being one of a small group at home to being one of a large class group at school. The Local Authority, for its part, has an obligation to provide full-time education for a child of compulsory school age whatever its previous educational background or experience, unless the child has special educational needs, in which case the provisions of the 1981 Education Act would apply.

COST AND QUALIFICATIONS

Parents do not need teaching qualifications to teach their children at home. The cost has to be measured in two ways. To educate children successfully at home at least one parent will have to forgo paid work. There will also be the cost of providing books and materials, although EO parents report that it is possible to take children up to GCSE in science subjects without vast expense on equipment. And of course all families have exactly the same access to libraries, sports centres, swimming-pools, radio and television programmes, and home computers. The only difference is that EO families will probably make much more intensive use of such facilities than those whose children are in school most of the time.

METHODS

There is no single method of teaching children successfully at home, although many members of Education Otherwise say that their 'bible' is *Teach Your Own* by John Holt, a much loved and lamented American advocate of a freer education for children. John Holt argues that most parents who take their children out of school do it not for philosophical or political reasons, but mainly to save them from the harm the school system is doing them. And he is a strong advocate of learning rather than teaching, arguing that real progress is made on the basis of children's enthusiasm, not with formal teaching methods and schemes of work.

Even so, most Local Authority advisers who keep an eye on the progress of children being educated at home will probably want some evidence of a coherent programme for children's development, particularly in the basic skills of reading, writing and mathematics, even if this does not closely follow what might be taught as part of the school curriculum – now the National Curriculum.

The methods used depend upon whether the family is concerned that children should gain formal qualifications, even though they are learning out of school, or whether they reject the competitive, qualification-oriented approach of traditional schooling, particularly at the secondary level. In practice many families seem to start off with a school-based approach, with so many hours a day set aside for 'lessons' and a formal programme of study for each week or month. Later, however, as parents gain in confidence, they feel more able to allow children to learn what they wish to at their own pace. The greater flexibility of home schooling means that when an interest extends outside the 'classroom' immediate advantage can be taken of whatever is available in the neighbourhood or even further afield. Teaching 'aids' can include the local countryside, museums and libraries, visits to places of interest, as and when needed.

One parent, quoted in the Education Otherwise introductory book *School is Not Compulsory*, put it this way:

'Our timetable is not rigid; enthusiasm is encouraged in any area of learning or interest and we continually seek to extend our awareness and knowledge. Whereas we had initially tended to clockwatch and were anxious if we found that we had diverted from world geography to current affairs and politics or from angles and tangents to aerial navigation, we now are excited by our sons' inquisitive minds and ability to encompass a vast range of topics. I frequently find difficulty in tearing myself away from a subject of which I earlier had scant knowledge.'

This is far from unusual amongst EO parents, who generally acknowledge that educating their own children involves an extension of their own education as well.

Parents of children who have been to school and been unhappy there do report, though, that it can take some time to revive an interest in learning if it has been damaged earlier. As another EO parent put it:

'I remember the first year of home education as being extremely trying as I battled with a child who had no interest in any formal work. I soon came to find out that most of what children are expected to do is quite meaningless to them and indeed is a great imposition on them. Very little is learnt from within and no sense of self is developed or indeed encouraged.'

There can be problems, of course, not the least reported by parents being sheer tiredness as they devoted themselves to their children's education for seven days a week. It may take some time if children have been withdrawn from school to settle into a new pattern of living and working together at home. One solution may be for parents to have one day 'off' a week, perhaps arranging to share child care and 'teaching' with another family, if there is one in the immediate neighbourhood.

Education Otherwise publishes two booklets of practical guidance on curriculum and methods for home learning families, *Early Years* and *The Later Years*. The latter includes advice on how to study for and take GCSEs, A Levels and other examinations at home, how to present a suitable secondary curriculum to the Local Authority, and how to teach secondary subjects such as foreign languages and science at home. It advises on the different correspondence courses available, and on where to obtain educational supplies and publications which may be needed for secondary work.

Education Otherwise can be contacted at 25 Common Lane, Hemingford Abbots, Cambs. PE198 9AN.

10

SECONDARY SCHOOLS AND THE NATIONAL CURRICULUM

KEEPING IN TOUCH – TO WHOM TO TALK

Links between home and school do not become any less important when children move up to secondary school, but they may become harder to maintain. You may no longer need to take or collect your children any more. And almost inevitably they will no longer be taught by a single – and easily approachable – class teacher, but by an increasing range of subject specialists, one for maths, one for English, and so on. However, all secondary schools should let you know the name of one teacher whose job includes the business of keeping you informed about what is going on in school, how your child is progressing, and who acts as the first port of call when you need help, advice or information. In most schools this is the class or form teacher – who may be assigned to your child's group for the whole of their school career, moving up with them each year. Or your child may be assigned to a tutor each year who will take responsibility for pastoral care as well as teaching. Or the head of year may be the person designated to deal with parental queries in the first instance. This member of staff will refer you on to other teachers, or possibly to the head, if that is necessary.

THE CHANGING CURRICULUM

The 1988 Education Reform Act introduced substantial changes in the school curriculum which will be fully introduced throughout the early 1990s in all maintained schools, including grant-maintained schools. The National Curriculum does not apply to City Technology Colleges, which are to have a more technological and vocational bias, or to the private schools, although it is expected that many private schools will follow the State sector closely, because their parents will demand the same assessment tests at seven, eleven and fourteen.

The National Curriculum consists of three core subjects: maths, English and science, and seven foundation subjects: technology, geography, history, physical education, art, music, and a modern foreign language. Religious education remains compulsory, and in Wales all schools must teach Welsh. The National Curriculum subjects must all be taken right up to the school-leaving age of sixteen.

What this means in practice is that over the next few years schools will be phasing out the option schemes that most have run for their fourteen-year-old pupils, allowing them to 'drop' some subjects and specialize in others which may either interest them more, or in which they hope to gain the best possible examination results. It is not yet entirely clear what flexibility will remain for pupils to specialize in certain subjects for GCSE. It looks unlikely that there will be space in the timetable for more than one subject in addition to the basic National Curriculum after the age of fourteen. But however the details work out in practice, the effect of some parts of the proposals are already clear.

In years one to three of secondary education the National Curriculum subjects are expected to be taught 'for a reasonable time' to all children up to the age of fourteen. For most schools, this will not prove particularly difficult, as they will have been teaching most of them to eleven, twelve and thirteen-year-olds anyway. The most obvious points of difficulty will be over Welsh in Wales, where not all schools have up until now made the national language compulsory, and enough qualified teachers may not be available, and over a modern foreign language. Some schools have exempted less able children from foreign language learning even at the early age of eleven or twelve. Unless children are such slow learners that they have applied for exemption from parts of the National Curriculum, they must all be included in language lessons from now on.

'Technology' is also an area of potential difficulty in some schools as the subject, as defined by the Government's working-party, embraces a whole range of 'subjects' such as design technology, art and design, home economics, information technology (working with computers) and craft subjects such as woodwork. Some schools have included all their children in this whole spread of subjects. Those which have not, and particularly those which may have encouraged a split in subjects between girls and boys, which strictly speaking is illegal, will have to change their practice. This may be particularly difficult for single-sex schools which are not equipped for the crafts and other specialisms usually associated with the opposite sex, i.e. workshop crafts or electronics for girls, and home economics for boys.

Beyond the age of fourteen, the introduction of the National Curriculum becomes even more problematic, because traditionally most pupils have studied only eight or nine subjects for examinations at sixteen, and they must now take ten (or eleven in Wales), and ten, moreover, which include elements of many more, plus, of course, compulsory religious education.

How this is to be done is still somewhat mysterious, with civil servants at the Department of Education and

Science talking about the 120 per cent timetable, which is apparently not such a contradiction in terms as it sounds if it is accepted that some 'subjects' will now be integrated into other areas of the curriculum instead of being treated as separate entities. Some subjects will disappear entirely as separate entities: schools will vary in their approach, but it seems likely that mainly craft or skill-based subjects like woodwork, metalwork, typing, needlework, and home economics will no longer be available as examination subjects. This does not mean that pupils will not be able to learn these skills: simply that they will be integrated into other parts of the timetable, particularly science and technology. And these and other subjects will be more likely in future to be taught in 'modular' examination syllabuses, which enable students to take elements from a range of subjects, art, music and drama, for instance, under the heading of creative arts, or history, geography and economics, under a humanities 'umbrella'.

Some elements of the National Curriculum picture are already clear.

'BROAD AND BALANCED SCIENCE'

Many parents will have been taught science as three separate subjects: physics, chemistry and biology, and many may have had difficulty in deciding at the age of fourteen which to keep on with and which to drop. Taking all three sciences up to O Level/GCSE usually took up 30 per cent of the timetable, and very often squeezed out other subjects such as humanities, languages or the arts. The whole aim of the National Curriculum is to reduce that 'squeezing out' effect and ensure that all children maintain their studies across a broad range of subjects. And the first and most welcome (in the view of most professionals) casualty is the teaching of separate science subjects up to sixteen.

In future all schools must offer a GCSE option, worth two conventional subjects, in science, which will include elements from all three of the specialist subjects. This will take up about 20 per cent of the timetable. There was great professional pressure from science teachers to make this the only option available. However, the Secretary of State decided to allow schools also to offer an alternative GCSE option, worth a single subject credit and taking up about 12.5 per cent of the timetable. It is still up to school governors to opt for 20 per cent science for all, and it is already clear that some schools will do so.

The 12.5 per cent science option, if it is available, should be looked at very carefully by parents. The experts in science education, who strongly opposed the Secretary of State on this issue, and equally strongly supported the idea of compulsory 20 per cent science for all, have two main fears. The first is that the 12.5 per cent option will be regarded as suitable for less able children, thus allowing them to gain a less extensive knowledge of science and fewer skills in this area than their brighter contemporaries, in spite of the fact that British industry is crying out for workers with better developed scientific and technological skills.

The second danger is that girls, who traditionally have shied away from the physical sciences like physics and chemistry, will be tempted to take the easy option again in future, leaving them with a balanced science qualification at sixteen which will not be enough to qualify them to take any single science subject at A Level. The lack of a credible science qualification at sixteen will also shut off any young people who take the single science GCSE course from many, if not most, careers with a scientific or technical base which recruit straight from school. So a National Curriculum which should have ensured greater equality for girls and the less able, in the competition for well-paid jobs, looks like leaving many of them just where they were before the legislation of 1988 was passed.

The National Curriculum Council has recommended seventeen attainment targets for science teaching. These will cover the following:

1. Exploration of science
2. The variety of life
3. Processes of life
4. Genetics and evolution
5. Human influences on the earth
6. Types and use of materials
7. Making new materials
8. Explaining how materials behave
9. Earth and atmosphere
10. Forces
11. Electricity and magnetism
12. The scientific aspects of information technology, including micro-electronics
13. Energy
14. Sound and music
15. Using light and electro-magnetic radiation
16. The earth in space
17. The nature of science

All these targets would be covered in a 20 per cent double science course for GCSE. A 12.5 per cent course would drop targets 2, 5, 7, 12, 15, 16 and 17.

TECHNOLOGY

Technology, as defined by the National Curriculum working-party, is a strange animal, and it is by no means clear how young people will in future gain GCSE qualification in the subjects that are included in this area. In the past, 'technology' has been used to describe the group of subjects taught as Craft Design Technology in most schools: a subject which involves the application of crafts and more modern skills, such as electronics, to design and problem-solving activities of all sorts.

As mentioned earlier, technology as defined in the National Curriculum also includes traditional subjects such as home economics, business and computer studies, art and design, and information technology, many of which were previously taken as GCSE subjects in their own right. It seems likely that many teachers who currently teach a single 'subject' in this area will in future find themselves teaching across a wider range of topics, and that in the later years of secondary education, these subjects will be dealt with in some sort of modular part of the timetable, where credits in individual subject areas add up to a qualification at sixteen.

The interim report of the technology working-party says that design and technology teaching and tasks may arise in a whole variety of school and out-of-school contexts: from the school itself, the home, factories and workshops, shops and farms. They do not include craft skills in the subject title but say that these will be needed by pupils, and will be acquired during a range of subjects across the curriculum. At secondary level, they say, contributions to technology could come from science, maths, geography, history, art and design, business subjects, CDT, home economics and information technology. What will be needed in future is some co-ordination of these different areas to ensure that pupils gain a coherent and comprehensive experience as part of the National Curriculum.

They propose four attainment targets:

1. *Identifying needs and opportunities*
   Pupils should be able to identify and state clearly needs and opportunities for design and technological activities through investigation of the contexts of home, school, recreation, community, business and industry.

2. *Generating a design proposal*
   Pupils should be able to generate a performance specification and explore ideas to produce a design proposal and develop it into a realistic, appropriate and achievable design.

3. *Planning and making*
   Pupils should be able to prepare a plan to achieve their design and to identify, manage and use appropriate resources, including knowledge and processes, in order to make artefacts, systems and environments.

4. *Evaluating*
   Pupils should be able to develop, communicate and act upon an evaluation of the processes, products and effects of their design and technological activities and those of others, including those from other times and cultures.

These targets are the basis for detailed statements of attainment for pupils at the ten levels of the National Curriculum. For instance, five-year-olds at Level 1 will be expected, under attainment target 4, to be able to describe to others what they have done and how well they have done it, and describe what they like and dislike about familiar artefacts, systems and environments.

At Level 5, pupils will be expected to be able to justify the materials, components, procedures, techniques and processes they have used in a project, and indicate possible improvements. They will also be expected to be able to evaluate the results of their work in relation to the original needs and opportunities, taking into account users' views, cost-effectiveness and the scale of production.

In purely practical terms, the working-party suggests, the average fourteen-year-old, for example, should be able to use a range of hand and powered tools and equipment – a plane, airbrush, cooker, database and spreadsheet, and a sewing-machine. They should be able to understand their function, the need for safety and the need to leave them in a fit condition for future use. They should know how to prepare the tools for use, and should know, for example, how to set the tension on a sewing-machine. And they should be able to use the tools to a level of precision and finish – setting in hinges to a box lid, for instance, or inserting a concealed zip.

The working-party accepts that design and technology is a 'new departure' for many schools, that it will need in-service training for teachers if it is to work successfully, and that how it works out in practice will vary from school to school as head-teachers make use of the expertise of their existing teachers, and are able to enlist the help and support of outside personnel and agencies, for instance from local industry and commerce.

LANGUAGES

When the National Curriculum is fully implemented all students will be expected to continue with the study of a modern foreign language up to the age of sixteen. At the moment 60 per cent drop languages at the age of fourteen when they make their GCSE option choices. And some schools exempt from a foreign language children who arrive in secondary education with severe difficulties in reading and writing English on the grounds that it is more important for them to spend the time on boosting their competence in English.

There are three difficulties for schools inherent in the new language policy which parents should be aware of. The first is the serious shortage of language teachers which already exists. It is possible that schools will not be able to recruit enough staff to implement the National Curriculum requirements at first. Some Local Authorities are already advising their schools that where there is a shortage of teachers they will have to draw up priorities for language classes: top priority must go to examination classes for GCSE and post-sixteen qualifications, attention must then be given to basic teaching of a language to eleven to thirteen-year-olds, then the possibility of offering a second language to pupils with particular aptitude should be considered, and only then should teacher time be spent on ensuring that classes for non-examination groups of fourteen and fifteen-years-olds are provided.

The second difficulty is over the type of teaching which will motivate children who find learning a foreign language difficult or boring: in other words, those children, including many of the less able, who drop languages now with relief at fourteen, or who have never until now been required to take them at all. Teachers who have only taught languages beyond fourteen to pupils who have chosen to continue studying them – and who may therefore be assumed to be reasonably well-motivated and interested – may find it very difficult to extend their teaching to less-motivated children.

The third area of contention is over the status of non-European community languages which are being taught in schools in areas which have significant ethnic minority populations. The assumption initially was that 'a modern foreign language' would normally be French or German, although presumably in areas which have substantial Italian or Greek communities there would be no objection to Italian or modern Greek being taught. However, the DES has now made allowance for community languages such as Punjabi, Urdu, Arabic or Chinese, for instance – where there is demand – so long as one of the other eight European Community languages is also taught.

WELSH IN WALES

The effect of the National Curriculum insistence that all

children in Welsh schools must now learn Welsh – either as a core or a foundation subject – will be to exacerbate the shortage of teachers of Welsh, and of teachers of other subjects who need to use Welsh as the medium of instruction. More generally, it will increase the pressure on the fourteen to sixteen timetable by pushing up the number of compulsory subjects which have to be taken from ten to eleven – plus RE. The possibility of taking any non-National Curriculum option at fourteen in Wales looks pretty remote.

HUMANITIES AND SOCIAL SCIENCES

The only subjects in this area guaranteed a place on the timetable once the National Curriculum is introduced are history and geography. Some element of both these subjects must be found a place in the timetable of all children up to the age of sixteen, regardless of whether they intend to take one or both, or neither, as a GCSE option. In practice it is clear that the only way that these two subjects can be included for most pupils is as part of some sort of modular or integrated programme of study which may also include elements of economics, politics and social studies, which are being pushed as essential areas of the curriculum by the other major influence on secondary schools, the Technical and Vocational Education Initiative. The DES has now conceded that development on these lines is acceptable.

TVEI was launched in a limited number of Local Authority areas – with generous funding – by the Manpower Services Commission in 1983 in an effort to improve the technical and pre-vocational skills of school-leavers. It undoubtedly gave an enormous boost to courses in science and technology, specialized areas like electronics and robotics, catering and food science, and business studies, all topics which proved highly motivating to the young people involved, although there is not much evidence that the courses actually improved examination success. TVEI, latterly under the aegis of the Employment Department, the MSC having disappeared, is now supposed to be extended to all pupils in all schools – and provides a different, and in some respects wider, influence on the content of the curriculum.

Elements of TVEI practice will surface right across the curriculum, as well as in specific areas like technology, but it may also have an influence upon how the humanities area is put together, because of its requirement that social, environmental and economic awareness be promoted.

Schools have still to work out in detail how this area of the curriculum will work in future. Parents will want to be assured that if history and geography, economics and any other of the social sciences, are taught in modular or integrated schemes, the level of attainment will be sufficient in any individual area to enable a student to go onto an A Level course afterwards.

However the timetable is arranged, there is going to be debate about the actual content of the curriculum in this area, both about the sheer amount of factual information which is taught, and about the balance between, say, national, world and local historical topics. The Secretary of State has gone on record as saying that there should be particular emphasis on British history – and indeed that children are not properly educated unless they do understand how the British arrived at their present international, cultural and political status in the world. But many historians also argue that there should be an important place in syllabuses for pupils to learn about the immediate local history of their own family, city, or region, and that it is more important than ever for young people to understand world as well as just national historical movements which affect us all: how Communism as well as capitalism, nationalism and internationalism, Zionism and Islam as well as Christianity have come to affect all our lives.

It is not only the factual content of history which has already proved contentious in some schools as the GCSE examination syllabuses have moved away from a mainly factual approach to the subject to one which emphasizes the skills needed to identify and assess the sources of historical material and draw conclusions from it. The point being made by historians generally, and by many school historians as well, is that there are many sources of historical evidence, very few facts are beyond dispute, and that reactions to events, and the conclusions drawn about them, vary according to the viewpoint of the observer both at the time and now.

To use a simplistic example, the historical and contemporary view of the slave trade, or the conquest of the far West of North America, may vary widely according to whether it is looked at from the point of view of a European, a European settler in North America, an indigenous African or a North American Indian. Similarly, the benefits of the expansion of the British Empire in Victorian times might seem very different to a Briton of Indian or Pakistani extraction from that of a white Anglo-Saxon whose family served in the Indian Civil Service. Even now the colonization of the Northern counties of Ireland by the British is a fiercely contentious issue within the British and Irish States. A modern historian, even at school level, would want to look at the evidence about the effects of these events from all sides of the racial, cultural, social and geographical divides. And many educationists would argue that this is even more important than ever in a world where travel, the migration of large numbers of people, and changing international relationships such as those brought about by the establishment of the European Community, are making the world a smaller place and individual nations more culturally, racially and religiously diverse than ever before.

Some of these issues of content, viewpoint and the handling of controversial issues will arise in other subjects in the humanities and social science area. Parents should be aware that the 1986 Education Act specifically enjoins schools to teach controversial issues without bias, taking into account that in many areas there may be more than one point of view, and that teachers should not impose their own views upon pupils.

Such controversial areas can arise in almost any subject these days – in teaching about the social and economic effects of science and technology, for instance, as much as in more obviously controversial subjects such as politics, economics and history. And the divisions of opinion do not necessarily follow simple party political lines: views on the new 'green' environmental issues, which might arise in geography, social studies, science or technology lessons, do not fall into easy party categories. Nor do contentious issues like abortion, contraception and sexual morality, which could also arise across the curriculum from religious education and personal-guidance lessons, to science classes. The requirement for balanced teaching applies to them all, and parents should approach the school if they feel that any subject is being given any particular political – or any other bias. All viewpoints are entitled to a fair hearing, and that includes those which advocate radical change, as well as those which wish to preserve the status quo.

THE ARTS
Art and music are now compulsory subjects up to the age of sixteen, although it seems that they will only be allocated a very small part of the timetable after fourteen, except for pupils who wish to take either or both as

examination subjects. When the National Curriculum was published there was concern that its designation of only two arts subjects as compulsory might spell the end of other creative options like drama and dance. To some extent drama may be covered as part of the English syllabus, but drama teachers argue that this does not allow its development as a creative, rather than an academic activity. Some schools are proposing to get around this potential restriction of the timetable by offering arts subjects on an integrated or modular basis so that time can be found across a year for all of them. This may mean that pupils with a particular talent for one of the arts may receive less teaching than formerly, and parents should make sure that any integrated course allows gifted musicians, actors or artists enough school time to develop their talents fully.

RELIGIOUS, MORAL AND PERSONAL EDUCATION

Religious education has been a compulsory part of the school curriculum ever since the 1944 Education Act. Indeed, until the passing of the 1988 Act it was the only compulsory part. The 1988 Act re-affirmed the duty of schools to include RE in all children's programmes of study right up to school-leaving age at eighteen, unless their parents have asked for them to be exempt on grounds of conscience. If you do want to withdraw a child from RE you must inform the head-teacher in writing.

The 1988 Act changed the law to make it obligatory for RE syllabuses to reflect the fact that British traditions are 'in the main Christian'. This had led to some confusion in the schools which have, in any case, to teach the syllabus agreed between the main denominations locally. Many of these syllabuses have over recent years begun to reflect the fact that Britain is increasingly a country of more than one faith, and that it is in the interests of cultural and racial understanding for communities of different faiths to learn to understand each other in school. Local Authorities must in future set up a Standing Conference on Religious Education, which will include representatives of all the major faiths, including the non-Christian ones, and which has the duty to revise the agreed syllabus for its area if requested to do so. This is a process which will take some time, so in the short term there is unlikely to be any change in how RE is taught.

In secondary schools, RE is often taught as part of a programme of personal and social education, which may also include elements of moral, health and careers education. Such an approach does not exempt a school from teaching the agreed RE syllabus.

The TVEI extension is particularly insistent that young people should have access to personal and social guidance at school, and to individual counselling on subjects like career-choices where this can be arranged and is appropriate. So early fears that this part of the secondary curriculum might be squeezed out by the academic emphasis of the National Curriculum so far appear to be unfounded.

OPTIONAL SUBJECTS

The National Curriculum will sharply reduce the number of optional subjects which students can study for GCSE, but depending on how individual schools interpret the new legal requirements, there should still be scope for one or two optional subjects for students who can cope with a total of nine or more GCSE courses. It is in this five or ten per cent of 'spare' time left over after the National Curriculum requirements have been fulfilled that a school should be able to provide scope for students who wish to take a second modern language, or classics, or art and music, to GCSE level.

11

GETTING THROUGH EXAMS

NATIONAL ASSESSMENT

The 1988 Education Act introduced a new national assessment scheme which will be compulsory for all children in maintained schools, including the new grant-maintained schools, at the ages of seven, eleven, fourteen and sixteen. This is not a new system of examinations in the traditional sense, for which parents can help to prepare children. The best guide to whether a school is helping children towards the appropriate level of achievement under the new system will be the programmes of study in the compulsory National Curriculum subjects. They will be the basis of the new assessment system.

The essential points to remember are these:

1. There will be ten levels of attainment. A five-year-old of average academic ability might be expected to achieve Level 1 after a year in school. A seven-year-old being assessed formally for the first time should reach Level 2 (a slow learner might still be at Level 1, a bright child at Level 3). The average eleven-year-old will be at Level 4, the average fourteen-year-old at Level 5 or 6, and sixteen-year-olds will reach Levels 6 to 10, which will be related to grades in the GCSE examination.

2. Assessment, particularly for younger children, will be by means of tests of skills administered by teachers as part of normal classroom activities. There will not be an all-or-nothing examination on a particular day, although written tests may be included in the assessments for older children.

3. Assessment tasks will be set nationally, and fit in with the programmes of study for the National Curriculum subjects. Assessment will be introduced first for English, maths and science.

4. The introduction of national assessment will be phased in, with pilot assessment of seven-year-olds in 1991 and the first full-scale assessment of seven and eleven-year-olds in three subjects in 1992. The first assessment of fourteen-year-olds in maths and science will follow a year later, and in 1994 sixteen-year-olds will be assessed in National Curriculum maths, science and English. Other subjects will be phased in up to 1997.

5. Assessment results for eleven, fourteen and sixteen-year-olds must be published for classes and schools. The publication of results for seven-year-olds is optional, but 'strongly recommended' by the Department of Education and Science. The results of individual children will be confidential to their parents and teachers.

6. When results are published, schools are also entitled to publish a description of their circumstances, which may illuminate why their results differ from others in the same area: for instance, they may have an unusually high intake of children whose first language is not English, or who come from disturbed home backgrounds, or conversely they may have an unusually high intake of children of high academic ability from privileged homes which encourage academic attainment. Factors such as these would normally explain some (not all) of the difference in results between schools of similar size.

GCSE AND NATIONAL ASSESSMENT: THE FUTURE
The first sixteen-year-old students took the new GCSE examination in the summer of 1988. Even before they

sat their examinations the Education Act, 1988, with its proposals for national assessment and the timetable which will be followed to introduce regular testing of all maintained school pupils, was on the statute book. The General Certificate of Secondary Education (GCSE) replaced GCSE O Level and the Certificate of Secondary Education examinations and itself took a full three years to plan and introduce, during which time school students were actually studying the new syllabuses and taking part in the new methods of continuous assessment which for many schools were very different from what went before. Although there were teething troubles with the new examination, particularly over its administration, it has been hailed by schools and the Government as a success and, as far as standards could be compared, has lead to higher levels of performance amongst sixteen-year-olds in the first two years. But with new plans for assessment following quickly behind, teachers in secondary schools, as least, could be forgiven for asking, as many of them did, whether this was not the straw that would break the camel's back. Could a teaching profession, which had worked extremely hard to make a success of GCSE in what was generally regarded as a very short time, cope with another major change in assessment so soon? And would the national assessment system at sixteen, just before the official school-leaving age, eventually make GCSE redundant anyway?

The answer to the last question is probably yes, but only in the long term. National assessment at sixteen will be introduced between 1994 and 1996. It will take even longer for employers and admissions tutors in higher and further education to familiarize themselves completely with the ten levels of attainment which the system offers and the fact that some of the attainment targets can be reached in more than one subject, i.e. some scientific skills could be assessed in science, in technology – which will include traditional areas like CDT, computer studies, home economics etc. – or even in geography. And it is possible to argue the other way around: that at sixteen the higher national assessment levels will be subsumed into the GCSE grading system. Work has begun at the Schools Examination and Assessment Council on that. What is clear, though, already, is that the new system and the GCSE share a common approach to assessment, one which emphasizes skills and practical applications as well as knowledge and understanding.

THE NEW EXAMINATIONS

GCSE

GCSE replaces the two previous separate examinations for sixteen-year-olds: O Level and CSE. It is organized by five examining groups which bring together the former O Level and CSE boards on a regional basis, although schools are free to choose courses from any of the groups. GCSE is an individual subject examination, although it is increasingly possible to take integrated or modular courses which lead to more than one GCSE pass, i.e. a double science award, or double humanities. The former will become even more common when the National Curriculum requirement that science must be taught on 'balanced' courses, i.e. including elements of chemistry, physics and biology, is enforced. GCSE is taken at sixteen. Older entrants take a special 'mature' examination.

HOW IS IT DIFFERENT?

GCSE differs from the O Levels many parents may have taken both in its teaching approach and in its methods of assessment. One aim of the examination is to increase students' practical skills and ability to make use of the knowledge they have acquired, and to reward them for what they can do rather than penalize them for what they don't know. GCSE courses, therefore, include a much greater emphasis on practical work in all subjects, from science and technology to maths and geography. English and foreign languages have increased the emphasis on oral work. And the emphasis has moved away from one all-or-nothing end-of-course examination in favour of different methods of assessment.

Students may be required to submit a sample of their two years' COURSE-WORK to the examiners. This usually means selecting the best out of a set number of assignments to send to the examiners. Many courses include extended PROJECTS or ESSAYS, which will be prepared over a period of time and which may well involve a considerable amount of individual research and preparation. These too will be sent away to the examiners. Other courses will include an element of CONTINUOUS ASSESSMENT, which means that the student's own teacher will mark work done during the course and assess it on behalf of the examiners. Examples of a class's work and of the teacher's marking will be MODERATED (or compared) by other teachers from other schools (or by examiners) before a final grade is arrived at.

Courses which include aspects of more than one subject: humanities, or the creative arts, or 'balanced' science, for instance, may have END OF UNIT TESTS on the completion of each section – often called a MODULE – of the course. The final GCSE grade will depend on the aggregate of two years' test scores. The difficulty with this type of assessment, and to some extent with continuous assessment, is that a student's standard of work should be expected to improve over the two years of the course, between the ages of fourteen and sixteen.

It is not yet clear whether the examination groups have completely solved the problem of allowing for this progression during a course which is assessed throughout the two-year period.

Most courses will also include some formal examinations or tests, but these will also be of a different kind. One of the ironies of the old system, its critics argued, was that it was possible to 'pass' O level with only 35 or 40 per cent of the marks: in other words, having mastered only about a third of the course, and failed the rest. The aim of GCSE is to set objective levels of achievement linked to the assessment grades which will indicate reasonably accurately what students can do at each level of attainment. This means that the 'pass' mark for a particular part of the course might be set high – say, 70 per cent – but the test will be pitched at the level students might be expected to have attained with, if necessary, different levels of difficulty for various types of student.

This means that it is necessary for schools to decide, in consultation with parents and students, which level of final examination students should enter for in some subjects. 'DIFFERENTIATED PAPERS' of this kind are most common in maths and some of the science subjects. It is a difficult decision for some borderline children because the possibility of attaining the highest grades may be confined to students who take the hardest papers, but it is also possible for students who do badly on the hardest papers to fail to gain any grade at all, even though they may have done reasonably well on less difficult papers. This is an anomaly which caused some distress in the first year of GCSE and to which the examination groups are attempting to find a just answer.

AS Levels
Advanced Supplementary Level examinations were

taken for the first time in 1989. They are intended to represent 'half' a traditional A Level, and become one of the acceptable qualifications for entry into higher education.

The notion of AS Levels grew out of the twenty-year debate about academic specialization by seventeen and eighteen-year-olds staying on at school or college in England, Wales and Northern Ireland (Scotland has always had a broader sixth-form course during which students study four or five subjects). The traditional concentration on three A Level subjects, very often confined to one area of the curriculum, i.e. all sciences, or all humanities subjects, has concerned educationists and employers for many years. In most other countries young people are required to keep a broader range of subjects, including maths and science, going until eighteen. In Britain there is particular worry that far too high a proportion of sixteen to eighteen-year-old students are dropping out of science and maths completely, and so remain unqualified for scientific and technological courses in higher education, whose graduates are in great demand by industry.

The idea of AS Levels as a solution to this 'narrow' post-sixteen curriculum was proposed by Sir Keith Joseph, Secretary of State for Education in 1984. He suggested that students who took A Levels in science could complement their studies by taking an AS Level in English or another humanities subject. Similarly, those keen to specialize in the humanities could take a balancing AS Level in maths or a science.

Schools and colleges took up AS Levels cautiously, and not always in the way envisaged. Some schools have chosen to put pupils in for AS Levels after one year as a sort of half-way stage to a full A Level. Many schools do not yet offer AS Levels, because they say they do not have the resources to sustain them. But their availability is increasing and has been boosted in two ways.

Firstly in 1988 the Higginson Committee, set up to look at the future of A Levels, suggested a switch to a five-subject sixth and seventh year curriculum, instead of the present three A Levels, so making it easier for students to follow a balanced diet. The Report was welcomed by higher education, the schools and by employers in industry and commerce, but turned down by the Government. As a result, many educationists began to look to AS Levels as a welcome existing means of encouraging sixth formers to take more subjects. From being an optional extra, AS Levels now look like being the main means of achieving a broader sixth-form course over the next five to ten years.

The potential of AS Levels as a credible qualification was also boosted by the Committee of Vice-Chancellors and Principals and other higher education organizations who quickly moved to make clear their acceptance of AS Levels as a valid qualification for higher education courses. The majority of universities and polytechnics now accept AS levels as an entry qualification, although, of course, individual entry decisions are taken by admissions tutors, some of whom may yet remain to be convinced.

CPVE

The Certificate of Pre-Vocational Education was also introduced by Sir Keith Joseph in an attempt to provide a credible qualification with a strong pre-vocational orientation for young people who wish to continue their education beyond sixteen but who are not attracted by, or are not capable of achieving, A Levels or vocational qualifications immediately.

The CPVE is not an examination at all: the certificate is gained by a course which combines elements of academic, practical, and social and personal education, and work experience. There is a common core divided into ten 'areas of competence', ranging from communication and numeracy to problem solving. There are five areas of vocational study to choose from, which will include work experience. And optional 'additional studies' may be creative or recreational.

The CPVE is validated by a joint board set up for the purpose by the two vocational examining bodies: the City and Guilds of London Institute and the Business and Technician Education Council (BTEC) and is available in further education colleges and some school sixth forms, and sometimes jointly in both. Syllabuses are drawn up to meet local needs, and what a particular student does to gain a certificate will depend on individual aptitude and interests. It will all be drawn together in a profile describing what has been undertaken and achieved rather than in terms of pass/fail examination results.

The CPVE is intended to lead on either to further academic work, such as A Levels, to vocational courses in further education, or to a job. But it is not yet clear to what extent employers have come to recognize the qualification, or how far BTEC, as the major provider of vocational qualifications, is committed to it as a stepping-stone to more advanced courses.

WHAT SUBJECTS TO TAKE

At fourteen plus

The National Curriculum, and the new legal requirement for all examination courses to be approved by the Secretary of State for Education, will gradually reduce the options open to fourteen-year-olds over the next few years. With a high proportion of the timetable taken up by the National Curriculum, most young people will inevitably take a majority of GCSEs in the ten core and foundation subjects. One or two others may be the only real choice there is.

In the meantime, while option schemes for fourteen-year-olds survive, there is much to be said for aiming to achieve a balanced curriculum so that as many career pathways as possible remain open when the examination results come out two years further on. Many fourteen-year-olds swear blind that they know exactly what they are going to do in adult life, and use that as a basis for making choices. Some are sadly disappointed when they change their minds about a career and find they do not have the qualifications they need.

Most schools make maths and English compulsory, and GCSE passes at grade A, B or C in English language and maths are essential for entry to many higher education courses and professional careers.

While it remains possible to choose separate science subjects, i.e. physics, chemistry and/or biology, it is possible to exclude yourself inadvertently from important areas of further study and career choice at this stage. Giving up physics at fourteen makes it virtually impossible to go into a wide range of scientific and technical careers, from medicine to electronics. A technological option at GCSE is also useful for some technical careers. In general, science and technology are harder to pick up again later if it is found that a mistake has been made. At eighteen, universities have been known to accept students with three science A Levels to read English literature. It is very much harder for someone with a collection of exam passes in arts subjects to switch back to science, particularly without GCSE in physics and/or chemistry, although some conversion courses are available.

As mentioned in Chapter 10, girls are particularly prone to opt out of the physical sciences and so close off a great many career options for themselves. It appears that even with the National Curriculum schools will be able to offer a condensed science course, taking only 12.5 rather than 20 per cent of the timetable. Many schools are worried that girls in particular will be tempted by this option, and so be unqualified at sixteen to take any science subject at A Level.

Many schools also recommend that all students should take at least one subject from the humanities – geography, history, religious education and the social sciences – and some also advise students to continue with a creative option as well to give even greater breadth. The National Curriculum supports this view by insisting on art and music to sixteen.

The final choice at fourteen has to be a balance between what students will succeed in, and what they enjoy most. Most schools organize a detailed consultation with parents about fourteen-plus options, and families should take every opportunity to consult subject teachers before decisions are taken.

At A and AS Level

A and AS Level options will be constrained by what a student is particularly good at – and many schools will ask for a specific GCSE grade as a qualification – and what the school can offer. As pupil numbers have fallen and sixth forms have become smaller, the latter consideration has become increasingly dominant. The DES recommends that a school's sixth form should offer at least fourteen A Level subjects. Sixth-form and tertiary colleges can often offer thirty or more, which gives some idea of the choice which is available in a big institution.

Even if, on paper, a school appears to offer a reasonable choice of A and AS Levels, appearances can be deceptive. Timetabling constraints may mean that subjects can only be taken in a limited number of combinations – maths with science subjects, for instance, but not with arts. The more unusual the combination requested, the harder it may be to meet in a small sixth form. Some areas have tried to get round this constraint by organizing co-operative schemes between sixth forms in neighbouring schools.

In theory this sounds attractive, as it allows schools to continue with a viable sixth form however low numbers fall, but in practice parents and students have often found that studying in two, or possibly three, different institutions simultaneously is not satisfactory. Close contact with teachers is lost and the great strength of the English sixth form, its close pastoral care, is dissipated as students spend all their free time travelling around to classes.

In some areas these schemes have proved so unpopular that they have accelerated moves to close school sixth forms and set up tertiary or sixth-form colleges instead. For an individual student, who cannot wait around for the whole local school system to be reorganized, an unsatisfactory sixth form offer may be the cue to look around for a larger institution to transfer to. At sixteen students can simply vote with their feet if provision is unsatisfactory, and move to another school or college.

EXAMINATION DISPUTES

There are two common causes of friction between schools and parents over examinations: the choice of subjects and the results.

Entering students for examinations costs schools money in fees, so they are understandably reluctant to enter students who have no hope of success. Great friction used to be caused when a choice had to be made between O level and CSE entry. With the advent of GCSE, there should be fewer disputes, although in some subjects there is still the question of differentiated papers to resolve. In extreme circumstances if parents think a student should enter for an examination and the school does not, it should be possible for the parents to pay for an individual entry themselves. This seems to offer a reasonable compromise.

Examination results which do not come up to expectations are a cause of family anguish every year. If a result is seriously awry – and particularly if the subject concerned is one which is significant for the student's future – parents should consult the school and discuss the result with the subject teacher. An examination board can only be approached about an individual entry with the support of the school or college involved. It is possible with that support to ask for the result to be checked – in which case the papers will be looked at in case there has been a simple error in the marking. Or a request for a full re-mark can be made, for which the exam board will charge a fee. A paper will not be marked down as a result of re-marking, but the examination boards say that in practice only a very small percentage are actually marked up. It is also possible for a school to ask for a review of results for a whole class if they think it has done particularly badly.

GRADED TESTS

There is one additional way in which some schools are testing children, although it is a method which may be superseded by the National Curriculum assessments when they are introduced at secondary level. Graded tests work on the same principle as traditional performing music examinations: a level of achievement is specified and students can attempt to reach that grade as and when necessary. There are no age limits. Graded tests have been developed in some Local Authority areas, particularly for use in 'linear' subjects like maths and foreign languages. Teachers and students like them because they spell out precisely what has been learned and give a sense of achievement which can be reinforced quite frequently as students work their way up the grades. Graded test results would normally be included in a student's profile or record of achievement on leaving school.

WHAT PARENTS CAN DO TO HELP

There are two basic rules for helping children cope with examinations, whether the test concerned is an entrance exam for a private school at eleven, or the major public examinations at sixteen and eighteen.

(a) Know what the student is expected to achieve.
(b) Provide all the support you can at home.

Neither of these injunctions is quite as easy as it sounds. Knowing what a student has to achieve to pass an examination involves close liaison with the child's school. Examination syllabuses are traditionally mysterious things, although they will be more easily accessible when the information requirements of the 1988 Education Act come fully into force. Parents may then ask to see examination documents.

It is not generally necessary, though, to sit with the syllabus beside you to supervise a child. It is well worth asking teachers, though, whether they expect to be able to cover the whole syllabus in the teaching time available – this is sometimes difficult, though not necessarily fatal so long as students are well aware of what they have NOT covered, and that they will not be able to attempt some questions.

With modern assessment systems it is even more important to know what students have to achieve throughout the course. Most courses for public examinations last two years, but few these days rely solely on a final examination. There are staging posts

162

along the way by which course-work must be prepared and submitted, projects finished and oral and practical assignments and assessments completed. For any GCSE course, in particular, the school should provide a time-table of important dates and deadlines to be met early in the course. Ask for one if it is not obviously forthcoming. It is particularly important that different subject teachers should liaise over deadlines, so that students are not expected to hand in several projects in the same week. It should be possible for the school to arrange some leeway for finishing off work, and still meet the examination group's timetable for submitting work. But meeting the examination group's deadlines is vital: failure to submit course-work or projects will lead to failure.

With all that information to hand, a parent's job is to provide the conditions in which a student can achieve the best grade possible in what is, at the examination stage, a stressful business. There are some basic essentials:

(a) Somewhere warm, quiet and well-lit to work (although a large number of teenagers insist on working to the sound of pop music without apparently impairing their performance!)
(b) The encouragement of a sensible regime of work, relaxation, sensible eating and sleep. This may require some patient family negotiation: all four elements are important and should be balanced, but teenagers do not always immediately agree. Lots of encouragement and some rewards for hard work will almost certainly be more productive than endless nagging.

HELP WITH COURSE-WORK

With the increased amount of weight being given to course-work and projects, there is some debate about the legitimacy of parents helping students who are working at home. The aim of producing a piece of course-work or a project is to present to the examiners the best work that the particular student is capable of. There is nothing wrong with advising students on where to look for information, on how to improve a draft, or on how to present work attractively, so long as the students actually seek out the information, read it for themselves, and made the suggested revisions on their own. Teachers will be giving this sort of help anyway, and should be aware that some students will get more help at home, and more access to information and books, than others, so that they can compensate.

The whole point about this sort of assessment is that the student is NOT expected to submit a first draft of a piece of work, as in a timed exam, but has time to improve and polish: this will be true for all candidates and will naturally be taken into account by the examiners. They will expect the spelling and presentation to have been checked. In fact some groups will accept word-processed work, which may have been checked by a computer spelling programme! They will not, though, expect the piece of work to have been effectively written by an adult, whether parent or teacher. Teachers will be looking out for undue parental influence on written work, and examiners will be looking out for signs of undue teacher influence when they mark batches of work from the same school. There is a delicate balance to be struck between advice, which is legitimate, and interference, which is not. If in doubt, discuss it with the subject teacher who should have a good idea what students are capable of achieving in their own right.

REVISION BOOKS AND AIDS

Some schools are notoriously short of textbooks and library books, and this is an area in which many parents feel moved to help their own children. There are an increasing number of series of revision aids – books, tapes and computer programmes – on the market, many of which are thoroughly researched, usually by practising teachers. Many young people find them a considerable help, because they usually explain topics simply, in a way which a busy teacher with an examination class may not have time to do for every individual child. If in doubt about which series is reliable, consult the subject teacher.

PRACTICAL HELP

Some points to remember:

(a) The examiners are interested in finding out what a candidate knows: it is always better to write down what you know about a question than try to pad out an answer with information that is not relevant.

(b) Psychologists say that nothing we learn is ever 'forgotten': the secret of passing exams is to unlock what is locked up in your mind at the right moment.

(c) The key to success is not memory but understanding, so if there is a topic which is not thoroughly understood, get help and make sure the understanding is there well before the stage of last-minute revision.

As the examinations approach use the following check-list:

1. Start revision in good time: nothing creates panic more effectively than the feeling that there is not enough time to get through everything.

2. As mentioned earlier, make sure that there is somewhere comfortable to work that suits the student, with or without music, with or without friends, at home or in the local library, etc.

3. Make sure that a reasonable amount of work is actually being done without cramming: there should

still be time for some leisure activities, and adequate sleep is vital. Working late at night is not a good idea.

4. Make sure the student has a coherent revision strategy: some people make lists, some make notes, some use cards, diagrams or drawings, in order to reduce a mass of information to chunks which can be handled. Remember memory is aural as well as visual, and that some people recall what they have heard more clearly than what they have read. Use tape-recordings if these help.

5. Try to lower the tension: GCSE and A Level years are tough for young people. Don't add to the stress by implying that all is lost if the results are not as good as expected. All is not lost: examinations can be retaken, new applications made for college places, alternative routes or careers can be considered. The education system is increasingly flexible.

6. When the exams approach, make sure that the candidate has been advised on exactly how to tackle the papers: reading the instructions carefully, dividing the time carefully between questions, with some time left for checking, and actually answering the questions the examiners have asked rather than the ones the examinees wish they had asked.

7. And on the day, make sure they have all the equipment they need: pens, pencils, erasers, calculators, dictionaries, if permitted, even a handkerchief. And make sure that they eat a good breakfast or lunch, take a few sweets with them, and go to the loo before they go into the examination room. It is possible to slip out, accompanied by an invigilator, but it is very distracting.

into a sixth form in their own school which will offer a range of A Level, and increasingly AS Level courses. This is the traditional route into higher education, and the choice of subject – even though it will be broadened by the introduction of AS Levels, worth 'half' an A Level each – is expected to reflect what students believe they would like to do after school: continue their education by taking a degree course or some other higher education course, or enter into one of the professions which normally recruit school-leavers at eighteen: banking, insurance, nursing, etc.

The choice of A-Level subjects, therefore, should bear some relationship to career or higher education intentions, if these are known. It is not entirely necessary, though, to have made crucial career decisions at sixteen – although it can be difficult to get into particular professions and courses if the wrong A Levels have been taken. A degree in physics, or medicine, or a foreign language is unlikely to be accessible if sciences or languages have not been studied in the sixth form. However, many young people of great academic potential genuinely do not know what career they would like to follow at sixteen, and in that case it is wise to choose A Level and AS Level subjects which keep options open. A third of sixth formers these days take 'mixed' A Levels, combining a science and/or maths with subjects from the humanities or social sciences. This is a good way of keeping a range of jobs and higher education courses open for a further two years.

In some areas, individual schools will not have sixth forms. A Level courses will be available in a sixth-form or tertiary college, which will generally provide a much wider choice of A Level and AS Level subjects than a single sixth form can offer.

Parents and students should be aware that as school numbers continue to fall, sixth-form numbers will also decline. Small sixth forms are often fiercely defended but they inevitably find it difficult to provide an adequate number of post-sixteen courses, and there is evidence that very small A Level classes – with perhaps only three or four students – do not provide the intellectual stimulation students need at this level of work. If there is a choice locally between A Level courses in a small sixth form and in a larger college setting, it should be investigated very carefully.

FURTHER EDUCATION COURSES

Further education and tertiary colleges (combining sixth-form and F.E. provision) offer vocational as well as academic courses. Some young people are better suited at sixteen to an educational course which leads more specifically towards working life: although following, for instance, the BTEC route to qualifications at eighteen, does not rule out the possibility of moving into higher education. It is an alternative route which the higher education institutions are increasingly coming to recognize, but which also provides qualifications for starting a career in industry and commerce at eighteen.

Further education colleges also provide the one-year pre-vocational CPVE course, and vocational City and Guilds and Royal Society of Arts courses in a wide variety of subjects. For a sixteen-year-old who is no longer motivated by the academic, subject-based approach of school work, the F.E. college may provide a much more satisfying means of continuing with education beyond school-leaving age – an increasingly desirable objective in an increasingly qualification-oriented society in which skills are at a premium.

HIGHER EDUCATION

Applications for places in higher education have to follow a complicated timetable which the head of sixth-form should advise on, because applicants require a reference from their head-teacher or principal. It involves applying to university through the Universities Central Council for Admissions (UCCA) and for most degree courses in the polytechnics and colleges through the Polytechnics and Colleges Admissions System (PCAS). Applications to Oxford and Cambridge Universities are dealt with separately, have to be made even earlier in the academic year, and may involve an entrance examination at Oxford. Places for school-leavers are usually offered on the basis of minimum A Level grades to be obtained, the required grades being decided individually by each admitting department. The rough pecking order is that very high grades – three As – are required for Oxbridge colleges, and for medical and veterinary courses; somewhere around three Cs are needed to get onto a university course in a less popular subject, and that it is possible to get onto a degree course in such subjects (i.e. science or engineering) in a less popular non-university college with two D or E grades. Details of the grades sought are increasingly available in prospectuses, and if not, in Brian Heap's annual survey: *Degree Course Offers* (see page 220).

Students applying before their A Level (or other) examinations will be made a 'conditional offer', which will probably be withdrawn if the grades required are not achieved. Both the university UCCA and college PCAS organizations use a system called 'clearing' to fit students with the minimum qualifications into the remaining available places after the A-Level results are published each summer. This can be a traumatic process, and one which leaves little time for considered thought about what is still on offer.

Several organizations have now computerized much of the information needed to understand the higher education system. ECCTIS (Educational Counselling and Credit Transfer Information Service) can provide information on all higher education and some further education courses, and the Higher Education Information Service, based at Middlesex Polytechnic, monitors courses in polytechnics and colleges of higher education.

It is possible for school-leavers seeking higher education places who do not succeed at the first attempt to try again. They can either resit their A Level examinations at school, at a further education college, or at a fee-paying college (often known as a crammer). Alternatively they can apply for a place the following year on the basis of the grades they have achieved the first time around, and use the intervening year to work or travel, or both. Many higher education tutors regard a 'year off' between school and university or college as an advantage, but some do not. It is worth consulting the colleges or universities to which applications are being made about their attitude.

For students who appear to have lost their way in the educational and careers jungle, parents can turn to one of the private vocational guidance services which will put the student through various aptitude tests and interviews and offer advice on appropriate courses of action. This can be expensive, and there is no independent vetting of the agencies concerned. The British Psychological Service will, however, provide a free list of its members who provide guidance services of this kind.

13

CHILDREN WITH SPECIAL NEEDS

Some parents do not need to be told that their child has a special educational need. Children with some physical disabilities, who are blind or deaf, or show signs of a severe mental disability, are very often diagnosed as young babies. The health and welfare service, and as the child grows older, the education service, are aware of the need early on, and can take appropriate steps to help the family.

Not all disabilities, however, are so easy to diagnose. The Warnock Committee, upon whose report the 1981 Education Act was based, estimated that at one time or another 20 per cent of children might have a special educational need. The need might be major or minor, permanent or temporary, but whatever the difficulty parents have an equal right to expect that the education service will offer constructive help. The concept of an 'ineducable' child was consigned to the dustbin of history by the Warnock Act, and a good thing too.

This does not mean that almost a decade after Warnock all families will find it easy to get appropriate educational treatment for their child when difficulties arise. The very first hurdle may be in diagnosing that a problem exists. A second major difficulty for families with children in difficulties is the sheer number of agencies and professionals who may become involved in their care and treatment: health, welfare, and education. The last hurdle will be finding a satisfactory teaching situation which will enable special-needs children to reach their full potential for learning. Resources for special-needs children are in short supply in some areas. Fortunately there are a large number of voluntary organizations which can offer parents help and advice. (See page 216.)

SPECIAL-NEEDS CHILDREN IN SCHOOLS

The Warnock Act decreed that children should be regarded as having special needs if they have learning difficulties which call for special educational provision to be made for them. This special educational provision may be provided in a normal school environment, although the Act did not suggest the complete integration of all special-needs children into mainstream education, as is often supposed. It accepted that some special schools, for children with particularly profound or complex disabilities, might always be needed. However, the Act placed on school governors the general duty to provide for special-needs children in their care. The Act does not apply to independent schools.

The Warnock Act's definition of children with special educational needs is that:

(a) They have significantly greater diffficulties in learning than the majority of their contemporaries, for whatever reason.
(b) They have disabilities which hinder them from benefiting from a normal education.
(c) They are under five and could fall into either of the above categories if they do not receive help.

Children in those three categories are entitled to special educational provision which is additional to, or different from, what the Local Authority provides for other children.

Local Authorities have a duty to ensure that special

educational provision is made for all pupils who need it. They must also ensure that children who have a formal statement of educational need are educated in ordinary schools, taking parents' views into account and – here's the rub – providing that their education in main-stream schools is likely to provide what they need, does not interfere with the education of other children and is cost-efficient. It is those last two provisos which sometimes lead to disputes between families and the LEA.

School governors also have a duty to ensure that special-needs children receive the additional help they require, that teachers understand the importance of identifying and providing for such children, and that everyone concerned with the child knows what those special needs are. The school must appoint a responsible person, usually the head-teacher, to make sure these requirements are carried out.

STATEMENTS

Most children with special educational needs will never be formally assessed. However, children with serious problems should be, in their own interests, and if a Local Authority believes a child over the age of two requires an assessment it can over-ride the objections of a parent. The purpose of an assessment, according to DES guidelines, is to seek 'a better understanding of children's learning difficulties for the practical purpose of providing a guide to their education and a basis against which to monitor progress'.

Once it has been decided that a child must be assessed there is a legal procedure which must be followed.

1. The parents must be informed in writing, and given details of the procedure, and the name of an officer who can be contacted for additional information.

2. The family has 29 days to appeal against the decision to assess. If the LEA changes its mind, it must inform the parents in writing.

3. Parents must be involved in all stages of an assessment, which must include educational, medical and psychological advice. They must be told of any examinations of their child and of their right to be present, and they can add their own evidence and comments. If they fail to send or bring their child for an examination they can be fined.

4. If as a result of the assessment the LEA decides to issue a Statement of Special Educational Need for the child, it must first of all submit a draft to the parents for comment.

5. The Statement has to include:

   (a) What the LEA believes the child's special educational needs to be.

   (b) What special educational provision the LEA believes will meet those needs.

   (c) The type of school needed and, if the LEA wishes to propose a school, its name.

   (d) The alternative educational provision proposed, if not in school.

   (e) Details of any other services or support to be provided by the LEA, Social Services or the Health Authority, to enable the child to benefit from the educational provision proposed.

   (f) The evidence, advice and information from the professionals and the parents upon which the assessment has been based.

6. The LEA may decide whether to issue a Statement, an amended Statement or no Statement at all in the light of the parents' comments on the draft.

7. If a Statement is issued, a copy must be sent to the parents with details of their right to appeal and the name of an individual to whom they may turn for advice.

APPEALS

Special-education appeals follow closely the normal school choice appeals procedures, but there is one important difference. The Committee can only confirm the LEA's decision or ask it to reconsider. It cannot back the parents' case. If an appeal is turned down, however, parents have a special right of appeal to the Secretary of State. However, it has to be recognized that in a dispute over a special-needs child, parents have fewer rights than normal. Appeals to the Secretary of State do not often succeed. And if it comes to a serious dispute over where a child should be educated, the LEA may enforce attendance through the use of a school attendance order. If a family is kept waiting for assessment or a school place, they have no similar power to make the LEA act on their child's behalf.

SPECIAL SCHOOLS

Special schools cater for children with particularly severe or complex disabilities. They include day and boarding-schools for primary and secondary age children. Most Local Authorities run some special schools of their own, which may or may not accept pupils from other areas, but there are also independent special schools, some run by voluntary groups specializing in the education of children with a specific disability, for instance the Spastics' Society and ICAN, the Invalid Children's Aid Society, schools.

Understandably LEAs generally prefer to educate special-needs children in their own schools if possible, on the grounds of cost. And parents who would prefer another school – particularly if it involves boarding at some distance – will soon discover that the provisions on school choice do not apply to special schools, so their rights in selecting a school are limited.

Disputes commonly arise over whether a special-needs child should board or not. An LEA may feel that a child will be best served away from home, while parents object. Alternatively parents may feel that a boarding-school will provide the best environment for a child, while the LEA baulks at the cost. Parents in this sort of dispute will need to produce evidence to back up their views. In the last resort they can appeal to the Secretary of State if they think the LEA is acting unreasonably.

INTEGRATION

Many parents prefer their special-needs child to be educated in a normal school if at all possible. The 1981 Act says that an LEA should meet this wish on three conditions:

(a) The child's needs can be met in the ordinary school.
(b) The education of other children in the school will not be damaged.
(c) It is compatible with 'the efficient use of resources'.

In practice a lot of LEAs still argue that proper provision cannot be made for many special-needs children in ordinary schools, and a family's desire for integration may run into official obstruction. Their best ally may well be a sympathetic head-teacher who is willing to take a child.

Some families, on the other hand, oppose integration because their child has already had a bad experience in a normal school or has even been excluded from one. In general, integration is not likely to work well unless the family, the child and the school are in favour of it and willing to put some effort into ensuring its success.

A family can appeal for a place in an ordinary school if they wish. But if the child has a Statement of Special Educational Need, they will have to prove that the school can provide what is needed, that the education of other children is not adversely affected, and that it will not cost the LEA more. Parents of children with special needs who do not have a Statement have the same right to choose a school as any other parents, and the same right of appeal if their choice is rejected.

SPECIAL UNITS

As a half-way house between special and ordinary schools, many LEAs provide special units attached to ordinary schools which specialize in the education of children with a particular disability, such as partial sight or hearing. Ideally children in such units should be integrated as far as possible with the main school, but this does not always happen.

Some LEAs also provide special units which are less clearly defined. They may claim to deal with 'disturbed' or 'disruptive' pupils who are referred to them either permanently or temporarily from ordinary schools. The Fish Report on Special Needs, commissioned by the Inner London Education Authority, was critical of the use made by some schools of such units – often referred to as 'sin bins' – and recommended that the criteria for admission should be made clear and that parents should be consulted fully if it is proposed to send their child to such a unit.

If a child is unable to attend school – either through illness or disability, or because of behavioural difficulties – the LEA may provide teaching at home or in a hospital or community home. This type of provision respects a child's right to an education, but is obviously not as satisfactory as education in school, if that can possibly be arranged. There are no DES regulations about what should be provided and the hours offered may be very short. Parents must be consulted if such an arrangement is proposed by the LEA.

THE NATIONAL CURRICULUM AND SPECIAL NEEDS

There are two particular worries about the way in which the National Curriculum might affect children and young people with special needs. The first concerns the use made of assessment results in comparing schools. If a school's quality, in an increasingly competitive situation, becomes dependent on such results, then there might be a tendency for schools to lose interest in integrating special-needs children, as the Warnock Act recommends. Children with learning difficulties might be seen as a drag on a school's results, pulling the average score down in a way which might damage a school's reputation. Organizations concerned with the welfare of special-needs children are very aware of this danger and are urging schools to continue to take a liberal attitude towards integration.

The second worry concerns the extent to which the programmes of study, and eventually the Standard Assessment Tasks, can be regarded as appropriate to special-needs children. There are two views on this. One welcomes the National Curriculum as a way of ensuring that all children – even those with learning difficulties – have a legal entitlement to the same curriculum. The other worries that for slow-learning children it may be demotivating to be constantly labelled as 'failures' as they proceed inevitably slowly up the ladder of levels of attainment.

The National Curriculum Council has said that it supports the principle of full participation for special-needs children in the National Curriculum, and the minimum use of the provisions in the Education Act which allow them to be opted out. The NCC says that it believes that the National Curriculum offers an opportunity to improve further on standards for special-needs children by guaranteeing them a broad and balanced curriculum. Nor does the Council see any reason why the introduction of the National Curriculum should lead to a rise in the number of formal Statements of Special Educational Needs. The requirement that special-needs children follow the National Curriculum will not be enforced until 1990, but the NCC has said that it hopes schools will introduce the new arrangements for their special-needs pupils as soon as possible, and that they will ensure that the assessment arrangements are implemented as sensitively as possible for children who will inevitably progress at a slower rate than normal, but who can still benefit from positive demonstrations of progress from year to year.

The Act provides that pupils with Statements may be excluded from the provisions of the National Curriculum or the provisions may be modified for such a child. In certain circumstances the head-teacher of a school may exempt any pupil from the National Curriculum, or modify its requirements, for up to six months. The head must inform the school's governors, the Local Education Authority and the pupil's parents, and if the parents object they have a right of appeal to the school's governors.

GIFTED CHILDREN

Children with outstanding talents are not included in the 1980 Education Act's definition of children with special needs, and so are not eligible for additional financial resources over and above what is provided as part of the normal school budget for children of their age in maintained schools. Many parents and teachers, however, agree that some extra provision needs to be made for some gifted children at least some of the time during their school career and there are various way in which schools attempt to meet these needs.

The most common in the early years of education is to provide all children with the means to pursue subjects in which they have a special interest or for which they show a marked aptitude beyond normal class-work. This may involve suggestions for additional reading at home, extended projects which take class-work a stage or two further, or the opportunity to study something completely different in school time, so broadening the curriculum for the most able.

In secondary schools, if a child is gifted in sport or a creative subject, there should be no barrier to following an interest at the child's own pace in lesson time, reinforced perhaps by extra coaching or homework or extended project work. In academic subjects like maths or a language, special arrangements may have to be worked out to enable gifted children to proceed at something like the pace they are capable of, even to the extent of allowing them to work for some of the time with older children. With the introduction of the GCSE it is harder for students to sit public examinations a year earlier than normal, which used to be what was done with O Level candidates. Course-work requirements and the need for a certain level of maturity to cope with some GCSE courses makes this option difficult. There is, however, nothing to prevent a school enabling children to extend their GCSE work, if they have the ability, or with helping them to take additional subjects – perhaps by means of a self-study course – if the normal curriculum does not seem to be sufficiently demanding.

What parents of a particularly gifted child have a right to expect is not the expenditure of significant sums of extra money on their child at a time when resources are short, but that school should be as flexible in dealing with the child of exceptional talent as they have often become in dealing with children with learning or emotional difficulties or physical disabilities. But parents should remember that although a child may be outstanding in one aspect of school work – maths, or art or languages –

he or she may perform at a very normal level in other areas, and be no more advanced in social or emotional terms than his or her contemporaries. Pushing gifted children too fast too soon can be counter-productive and emotionally damaging.

14

WHEN THINGS GO WRONG

PROBLEMS WITH PROGRESS

Parents of children of all abilities sometimes get into a dispute with a school because they do not believe their children are progressing as quickly as they should either in one particular subject or across the board. This may be difficult to resolve: a child's progress in school depends upon many variable factors – natural aptitude, motivation, the expectations of parents and teachers, and the class-teacher's ability both to maintain an orderly learning environment and to inspire children to produce the best they are capable of. The National Curriculum will give parents a much clearer idea of what to expect of children at different ages, but until that is fully implemented they are left to negotiate with teachers about what is appropriate and whether or not a child is falling behind what might be reasonably expected.

There are some useful questions that a parent might consider before asking to see a class-teacher or head about unsatisfactory progress.

1. Have the child's school reports indicated any deterioration in performance, in which case the school may be just as worried as you are.
2. Is the lack of progress confined to one area of the curriculum, especially at secondary level? It is not normal for a child to shine in most subjects and fall down badly in just one: if that is what is happening it may indicate inadequate teaching.
3. Is the lack of progress general? If so, it is reasonable to

try to work out whether the child is a naturally slow learner or whether there is some undiagnosed difficulty – poor sight or hearing, or dyslexia, or an emotional problem – which is holding the child back, or again whether the standard of teaching is generally poor. The school should have test results available on your child, and if it has not, it is quite reasonable for parents to ask for a test of reading, verbal and spatial ability. Such tests are not an infallible indicator of a child's potential but taken with other factors they are a help in diagnosing problems. In the last resort parents can approach the child-guidance service or an educational psychologist for help, including standard tests.

If you suspect bad teaching, have you discussed the difficulty with other parents with children in the same class who may be just as dissatisfied? One family may have exaggerated expectations of their own child, but if a group of parents are dissatisfied then they should be able to provide enough evidence to initiate a serious discussion with the school about what is going wrong and how it can be put right. Parent-governors should be willing to act as a link between parents with a grievance and the school. Teachers are the profess-ionals, and if parents are not satisfied with their child's progress they have a right to expect the child's teachers to come up with some practical suggestions for improvement – whether it is a special reading or spelling programme or, more drastically, a move to a different class.

The most highly charged disputes between schools and families often occur when a school refuses to accept that a child has a disability, such as dyslexia, which may be difficult to diagnose, or refuses to admit that a child is not making progress as quickly as parents have a reasonable right to expect, taking everything the school has to say about aptitude and test results into account. In the last resort, a parent has the right to move a child to another school if a vacancy can be found.

DISCIPLINARY PROBLEMS

Schools invariably impose a set of rules or a code of conduct on pupils, and parents have a right to see these rules, which should include the normal sanctions for unacceptable behaviour, such as detention. Any form of physical punishment is now illegal in maintained schools. Parents are assumed to have accepted the school's rules when they send a child to a particular establishment. The courts normally uphold the right of a school to enforce its rules – including those on dress – by means of sanctions – even if parents object to a particular sanction when it is imposed upon their child.

Occasionally parents have kept children at home in protest at some particular punishment or at the enforcement of a rule on school uniform or another form of dress. When such cases have reached the courts, as they inevitably will if a child is kept out of school for any length of time without good reason, the courts have invariably backed the right of the school to enforce its rules as it sees fit, so long as the sanctions used are reasonable. If parents have any objections to a school's rules or punishments it is therefore advisable to discuss them with the school before enrolling a child. As the law stands, schools also seem to have some limited right to enforce rules outside school premises, i.e. on the way to and from school, or when pupils are wearing uniform.

DETENTION

Detention is commonly used for minor breaches of school rules. Most school accept, however, that detention should not be imposed after school if it entails students missing a bus home or being put in any sort of danger after school. Most inform parents in writing if a student is to be detained and at what time the detention will end.

SUSPENSION

Schools have the right to exclude pupils for sufficiently serious reason in three ways:

(a) For a fixed period, for which the parents are given a definite date for return to the same school.
(b) For an indefinite period, in which case the pupil must remain out of school pending further investigation.
(c) Permanent exclusion, in which case the pupil cannot return to the same school but will remain on the school roll until a place can be found elsewhere.

A clearer definition of schools' rights to exclude pupils was a feature of the 1986 Education Act. Articles of government must now include:

(a) A clear outline of the powers of heads, governors and the Local Education Authority.
(b) A step-by-step guide to the procedure to be followed in each LEA area.
(c) Some safeguards against the arbitrary use of exclusion.
(d) An independent appeals mechanism for parents whose children are excluded permanently from a school.
(e) An independent appeals mechanism for governors in disagreement with their LEA and the head over an exclusion case.
(f) The right of appeal to the Ombudsman for both parents and governors who allege maladministration.

There is now a clear procedure for schools to follow when they wish to exclude a pupil:

1. Parents must be informed in writing of the exclusion without delay, and the reason for it. In the case of a fixed exclusion, they should be informed of the date upon which the pupil may return to school.
2. Parents must be told of the means of making representations to or making a formal appeal to governors and the LEA.
3. The head must inform governors and the LEA of any exclusion lasting more than five days.
4. In the case of a fixed exclusion the governors or appeal panel can direct the head to reinstate the pupil at an earlier date.
5. In the case of an indefinite exclusion, the governors or appeal panel can decide to direct the head to reinstate the pupil immediately or on a specified date; or decide not to reinstate the pupil at all.
6. If the governors do not issue a direction to reinstate the pupil at this stage, the LEA must do so. The head-teacher can then either comply with the LEA's direction, in which case the governors have a right of appeal to an independent panel, or the head-teacher can move that the pupil should be permanently excluded, in which case the parents have a right of appeal.
7. In the case of permanent exclusion, if the parent does not take up the right of appeal and the pupil is not reinstated, it is the responsibility of the LEA to make alternative arrangements for the education of the child.

Exclusion appeals will be heard by an independent committee set up under the 1980 Education Act on the same lines as those delegated to hear school choice appeals. The appeal should take place without delay, with parents being informed of the time and place in good time. Parents may make oral representations to the committee. Governors can make oral and written representations. The committee's decisions must be made in writing and are binding on the head-teacher, governors and LEA.

If, after an exclusion dispute, parents feel that their child would benefit from a transfer to another school, they may request a transfer, naming their choice of school, from the LEA. If the LEA does not agree, they have the same right of appeal as when a normal application for a school place is turned down.

TRUANCY AND OTHER ABSENCE FROM SCHOOL

Parents have a duty to see that their children are educated, and if a child is a registered pupil at school under school-leaving age, this means ensuring regular attendance. Schools are obliged to register pupils at the beginning of morning and afternoon school sessions, and if a child is absent repeatedly, or for a period of two weeks without a medical certificate or permission, the fact must be reported to the LEA.

Apart from illness, good cause for keeping a pupil away from school must concern the child, not the parent. In other words, a family emergency is not a good reason for a child to miss school. The law says that the child's education must take priority. Children may, however, stay away from school for recognized days of religious observance appropriate to the family, and if they are awaiting treatment for head-lice or other infestations. Older pupils will be excused school attendance if they are taking part in an approved programme of work experience, and families can seek permission to take a child away on the family's main holiday for not more than two weeks during term-time.

In secondary schools, and occasionally in primary schools, pupils may themselves play truant – with or without parental knowledge. A school's system of checking on absences should pick up truancy in its early stages, before it becomes a habit, and if truancy is suspected, parents should be contacted immediately. But truancy can come as a dreadful shock to parents if there has been no earlier clue that a child is unhappy at school and, for some other reason, not attending regularly. Truancy is very often a symptom of other problems at school: adolescent ones, bullying, learning difficulties, involvement in drug or solvent abuse or, in very rare cases, school phobia which makes it almost impossible for a child to attend school without very real distress.

SCHOOL ATTENDANCE

In cases of persistant truancy, the school will turn first to the Education Welfare Service whose responsibility is to liaise between schools and families whose children have problems. If all attempts to persuade a child to attend school regularly fail, the Local Authority may apply for a school attendance order, and if this still does not result in regular attendance, parents may be taken to court and fined, or even, in the last resort, imprisoned. The child concerned may also be taken into care on the grounds that they are not being educated. Parents facing this sort of serious difficulty over their children's education should seek legal advice.

In rare cases parents may be allowed to educate their children at home (see Chapter 9).

PERSONAL AND SOCIAL PROBLEMS

Most adolescents, and some younger children, experience difficult episodes during their school careers which may have an effect on their behaviour or their ability to learn. Schools generally regard personal and social difficulties as the province of teachers specializing in 'pastoral care' of pupils. This may be the form teacher or tutor, or the head of year. Some secondary schools also have student counsellors to whom pupils may turn for advice on personal as well as academic matters.

Primary and secondary schools normally include personal and social education in their curriculum, and they are aware of how closely school performance and children's emotional stability are linked. At secondary school, students will generally be advised on and discuss with teachers subjects such as personal relationships, sexual development and behaviour, and health education, including drug, solvent and alcohol abuse and smoking. If they have specific problems in these areas, teachers should be able to advise them on where to turn for private help and advice.

Similarly, parents who believe, or even just suspect, that their children have problems of this sort which may affect their school performance should consult the pastoral care staff. They should also make sure that the school is told of any problems which have arisen at home, such as a divorce or a bereavement, which may upset a child emotionally and possibly affect their behaviour or interfere with their school-work. Teachers will keep this sort of information confidential to those staff who need to know about it in their day-to-day dealings with the child. (See *Where to Get Help*, page 196.)

BULLYING

Bullying is one of the most insidious of school problems because however much misery it is causing to the victims, they are often unwilling to tell an adult about it for fear of being branded a 'sneak' or 'grass'. Misguided honour amongst children is often a very powerful force and the cause of great unhappiness.

Reluctance to go to school may be the first sign parents get that a child is being bullied, though surveys show that a disturbingly large proportion of children, when they are questioned closely, admit to having been bullied at some time at school. If a child is clearly unhappy about going to school, bullying is an obvious point to raise in discussions with staff. Some teachers are still reluctant to admit that bullying goes on in their schools – although this is an amazingly rose-tinted view of school life which has presented plenty of evidence of bullying from *Tom Brown's Schooldays* to the present occasional tragic suicides of youngsters who have been tormented at school. The Samaritans report that seven per cent of people who telephone them for help are under fifteen, and their greatest worry is about bullying.

Teachers do have a duty to prevent bullying in school and, as far as possible, on the way to and from school as well. Their duty extends to the abuser as well as the victim: no child should be allowed to grow up believing it is possible to bully younger, or smaller or weaker, people with impunity. It is not, as some adults argue, a natural or normal part of school life, and parents are entitled to help from the school if they believe their child is being bullied, or if they think their child is indulging in unacceptable behaviour of this kind. Parents should not run away with the idea that only boys get bullied. Girls can be just as cruel, and often in more subtle and hurtful way.

Some schools actually run an educational programme designed to discourage bullying. There are plenty of literary works, from *Tom Brown's Schooldays* by Thomas Hughes to the *Lord of the Flies* by William Golding, which can be used as the basis of discussion about the problem.

There are defensive measures that bullied children can take: they can stick with their friends when bullies are around (although the victim may often be the child without any friends); they can walk to and from home in the company of other trusted children, if possible older than themselves; they can avoid, if possible, the places where bullying often occurs – the school toilets are a favourite lurking place; and they can develop their own self-confidence and ability to stand up to physical threats, so making themselves less likely to fall prey to people on the lookout for victims weaker than they are themselves.

But the first line of defence for the victims of bullies has to be the adult community in which they live. If parents and teachers were more willing to talk about the problem, and make it very clear that aggressive behaviour is unacceptable, victims might feel more ready to come forward and complain. It is the victim's own silence which often leads to tragedy.

MAKING A COMPLAINT

The Education Act, 1988, lays down a formal procedure for making a complaint about the actions of maintained schools and Local Authorities in relation to the National Curriculum. It is expected that parents will first of all take up their complaint with the school staff in an informal way. If this does not resolve the matter, they have the right to complain to the school governors and finally to the Local Education Authority. If the complaint still remains unresolved, the Secretary of State for Education will be the last court of appeal.

The formal procedures by which complaints will be considered have to be drawn up by Autumn 1989, and details must be made available to parents under the information regulations of the Act.

The aspects of school affairs which will be covered by the complaints procedures are:

1. The provision of a curriculum, including religious education and worship, which meet the requirements of the Act.

2. The implementation of the National Curriculum in accordance with Government regulations.
3. The provision for pupils of compulsory school age of courses leading to approved external qualifications.
4. The provision of religious education and worship as required by the Act.
5. In the case of the LEA, the establishment of a Standing Advisory Council on Religious Education.
6. The need to act reasonably in deciding whether or not to seek exemption from all or part of the National Curriculum in order to carry out developmental work.
7. In the case of school governors, consideration of appeals by parents about the temporary withdrawal of pupils from all or part of the requirements of the National Curriculum.
8. The operation of changing policies in relation to the school curriculum.
9. Compliance with regulations about the provision of information.
10. Compliance with any other enactments or regulations concerning the curriculum.

WHERE TO GET HELP

There are various agencies within the educational systems to which parents can turn if their children are having problems at school. Most Local Education Authorities have an Educational Welfare Service, which would normally be the first agency involved if a child were playing truant, was persistently away through minor illness, or showed a sharp deterioration in performance or behaviour. The EWO advises parents on what help is available to them of a practical or advisory nature: grants for clothing, psychological services, etc.

Most areas are served by child guidance clinics and/or an educational psychology service run by the Local Education Authority or in some cases the District Health

Authority. Parents may ask for their child to be referred by the school, their GP, the Education Welfare Officer or may refer themselves by seeking an appointment. A child-guidance clinic might offer treatment on a regular basis for behavioural or emotional problems which might in some cases involve attendance by the whole family. An educational psychologist should be able to provide a professional assessment of a child's problems and potential. Both services are to some extent over-stretched by the demands of the 1980 Act on children with special educational needs, so prompt treatment may be difficult for parents to obtain.

There is also a growing number of private advisory centres; some, like the Dyslexia Association, concerned with one particular disability, others offering a more general advisory service – for a fee – on children's educational difficulties. Some useful addresses will be found in Chapter 18.

15

HEALTH AND SAFETY AT SCHOOL

Schools, like other places of work, must have a written statement of their safety policy under the terms of the Health and Safety at Work Act. The Local Education Authority is responsible for the safety of buildings and equipment. Most LEAs insist that schools hold a fire-drill at least once a term and this must be reported to governors. Anyone concerned about safety in a school can call in the Health and Safety Officer to look at particular aspects that are causing concern.

While children are in school, teachers legally assume some of the parents' duties in relation to the care of that child. The legal term is *in loco parentis*, in the place of the parent. This means that the school must take all reasonable steps to ensure the safety of children in their charge, and this has been quite strictly interpreted by the courts. The head-teacher is responsible for organizing adequate supervision of pupils at lunch-time or during morning or afternoon breaks, and this has been interpreted as meaning that play areas must be patrolled, either by teachers or supervisors brought in for the purpose. It is not enough simply to have a member of staff on call in the staff-room. Some head-teachers who have not found it possible to organize appropriate supervision at lunch-times have decided to close their schools rather than risk an accident on school premises for which the school or the Local Authority might be found liable.

The responsibility of teachers to supervise children extends to twenty-four hours a day if they take them on an educational trip or visit. And other adults who may accompany a school visit carry the same responsibility. Schools cannot disclaim responsibility for supervising any visit or outing which they have organized. Parents should be aware that under the terms of the new Education Act on charging for school journeys, the responsibility for organization and supervision of visits out of school time may pass from the school and Local Authority to the travel firm which undertakes the organization. They should inquire in future who is responsible for safety on a visit, and what insurance cover is provided for their children.

Educational visits organized by schools usually have to comply with guidelines on safety and supervision laid down by the Local Authority. These should specify the number of adults required to accompany children, and the qualifications adults must have to supervise outings which involve adventurous activities or hazardous locations such as mountains. Parents should be kept fully informed of what their children will be doing on a school outing or visit, to what extent older children will be allowed to move about unaccompanied, and what code of conduct will be enforced on matters such as bedtime, drinking, smoking, etc.

A school's supervision of a child lasts from a reasonable time before the school day begins, to the point at which school normally ends. If a school wishes to release children early or keep them later than normal it has a duty to inform parents so that safe arrangements can be made for children to travel home. The LEA has a duty to see that any transport it provides is properly supervised.

THE SCHOOL HEALTH SERVICE

Responsibility for school health lies with the District Health Authorities and what they provide varies from one area to another. The Department of Health recommends that all children should have a medical examination when they start school and at intervals afterwards. Parents should be informed if their child is going to be medically examined and given the opportunity to be present. Eye-sight and hearing checks are also usually carried out when children start school, and at intervals later, and parents will be informed if children need further investigation.

Children may also be inspected for infestation by 'nits' and can be asked to stay at home until the problem has been eradicated. Head-lice are very common and can be easily treated with lotions and shampoos. They are not a sign of a dirty home background.

INFECTIOUS DISEASES

Schools should be informed when a child is suffering from an infectious disease and the Local Authority has the right to exclude such children for a specified period. Notication of contact with German measles is particularly important because of the risk to pregnant women.

HYGIENE AND SCHOOL TOILETS

Children should be taught about the importance of good hygiene at meal-times and after visiting the toilet. Schools often find great difficulty in keeping toilets in a clean and unvandalized state, and parents should complain if there are problems in this area because of the risk to health. Toilets themselves should be kept clean and there should be adequate facilities to allow children to wash and dry their hands properly. School should be notified about stomach upsets because of the risk of contagion and the possibility that the school meal service may be involved in an outbreak.

16

EDUCATIONAL TOYS AND BOOKS

It is always said that lots of money does not bring happiness: it is even more true that lots of toys do not bring children contentment. How many of us have spent a fortune on Christmas presents for children only to see the very youngest sometimes having much more fun with the wrapping-paper than the present, and the older ones subsiding into sulks and tears as the day goes on and the novelty wears off some expensive gift.

So buying for children is an art – but fortunately it is an art which can be learned once it is realized that lasting pleasure is likely to come from something which stimulates a child's imagination rather than from a toy which, however expensive, leaves little room for children to experiment or create a world of their own. That's why the wrapping-paper and boxes prove so attractive to young children while the expensive contents may be thrown on one side: one sparks off the imagination; the other, sadly, doesn't. And if that is a lesson grandparents and aunts and uncles have to learn too, then it is never too early for parents to start – tactfully – to get that message home.

So how do parents, in the hurly-burly of the toyshop just before Christmas, which is the time of year when the vast majority of toys are bought, judge what is value for money and what is not?

There are basically four types of toy which children need for their development: those which lead to need for their development: those which lead to intellectual, emotional, physical and imaginative development. Some toys, of course, fall into more than one of these categories, but a simple rule of thumb is to check regularly that all four needs are being met by the range of toys available to your children. Some toys may be so large or expensive that they may only be available at a playgroup or nursery, or shared with brothers and sisters or friends. That does not matter. What is important is that they should be available for some of the time. It goes without saying that all four categories should be lots of fun as well. You cannot force children to learn through play. Given lots of opportunity they will do it all on their own.

TOYS FOR PHYSICAL DEVELOPMENT

Children learn physical control over themselves and their environment through practice. With babies and very young children endless repetition of simple actions enables them to pick things up and put them down and eventually control the finer movements of their fingers. Games and puzzles which involve fitting things together assist this process – with the control demanded becoming more sophisticated as children get older. Toys and games involving drawing, painting, modelling and 'making' all refine the hand-eye skills of older children, as well as extending their imaginations.

The development of the larger motor skills can also be encouraged by careful selection of toys, some of which can be expensive, but not all. All under fives love some form of locomotion, whether it is a pedal car or a toddler trike. Bats, balls, something to climb on or over or through, and later the introduction of more sophisticated ball-games such as catch, football and French cricket, lead to more sophisticated skills which a child's school will also be working hard to encourage.

TOYS FOR INTELLECTUAL DEVELOPMENT

It is difficult to think of any toys which do not fall into this category, because almost any toy will encourage children to think. But some will be more effective than others, and there are different sorts of thinking skills involved.

Obviously any toys or equipment which encourage drawing, writing and painting skills will aid children's intellectual development in a way which will be immediately applicable when they go to school. As they get older more sophisticated equipment will be required for use at school, but there is no reason why children should not also be encouraged to continue with these interests at home as well. They do not need to be especially talented: but they do need a supply of paper, pencils, pens and paints to enable them to improve their skills.

These days computers also fall into the category of educational toys. The National Curriculum is encouraging schools to make sure that even five and six-year-olds become 'computer literate', and there is no doubt that children with access to a computer at home do have an advantage over those without in this increasingly technological age. The question then arises, what are they going to do with the computer? Will they not simply waste a great deal of time playing fairly crude games? To which the answer has to be yes, they will almost certainly play games – but that does not really matter very much.

Most children in the 1990s will meet computers at school and later at work as tools to enable them to deal with procedures like the production of accounts, reports and the handling of data of one sort or another. The skills involved in word processing and data processing, which are what most people will need to do, are not in fact very complex. What is required, though, for them to be easily assimilated later when they are needed, is some confidence in using the technology: keyboards, monitors, tapes and disc drives. And some basic understanding of what a computer can and cannot do, never forgetting the old (in new technology terms) adage, 'garbage in means garbage out': in other words, a computer is only as efficient and effective as the person who programmed it.

Later on, some children will wish and need to take computer studies, and programming, to a much higher level. But they will always be in a minority. What the majority will need is familiarity and confidence to use the machines in everyday situations. And that can come through playing games as well as taking part in sophisticated educational programmes at school.

Slightly different abilities are encouraged by games and puzzles, ranging from simple six-piece jigsaws for toddlers, to Scrabble for the sub-teens who may be having trouble with their spelling. Toys involving sorting and matching are useful for developing mathematical skills. Games involving words are obviously useful for developing vocabulary and spelling abilities.

Mathematical, logical and spatial skills are also developed by the whole range of toys and games which can be loosely described as constructional. This is an area where girls are especially liable to be left out, as this range of toys is often regarded as particularly masculine. But just because Meccano and Lego are very often used to build machines of one sort and another by little boys does not mean that they can not be equally valuable as an intellectual – and an imaginative – stimulus for little girls. They may use them to create slightly different worlds for themselves, but the process is just as vital to their development as it is to their brothers.

TOYS FOR IMAGINATIVE DEVELOPMENT

All children learn from their own imaginative world as well as from real life, and this sort of learning needs to be nourished just as much as any other. By its very nature, though, it is much more difficult to predict just what children need to stimulate their imagination. It can be an elaborate contruction set, like Lego, from which children commonly create whole new worlds for themselves, complete with populations, rules and conflicts. Or it can be a heap of old junk which can be turned into a space craft, a pirate ship, a racing-car or a cave family's home at will. There is no predicting where the imagination will take children or what props will be needed to help them on their way.

So in this area, parents have to keep an open mind. Lots of toys for pretending with, from toy cars, dolls, animals, to construction sets, modelling and 'making' equipment, will all help. So will some dressing-up clothes, which can be family cast-offs just as well as expensive 'nurse' or 'space' sets from a shop. And on occasion the chance to 'play' with real-life equipment around the house in 'pretend' situations.

Tolerance and understanding of what is going on helps too, when the mess of imaginative play seems to overwhelm family good order and common-sense. Do not forget that children's ability to act our familiar situations helps them to understand the real world around them, and is particularly valuable in allowing them to come to terms with the conflicts of real life.

Do not be too worried about the violence of pretend play either. Normal children can distinguish very clearly between fact and fantasy, and need the latter very often to explore their own feelings and attitudes towards violence and conflict. It is often children who bottle up their emotions and are unable to express them even in play who cause serious concern later, which is not to say that an adult does not sometimes need to intervene if the 'play fights' look like turning into the real thing. It is a question of judgement.

TOYS FOR EMOTIONAL DEVELOPMENT

Children's emotional development is a difficult thing to measure. We all see our children becoming more mature, but it is often hard to see what has made the difference to their behaviour from one week to the next. It is also difficult to separate the toys and games which help children to develop emotionally from those which encourage their physical, intellectual and imaginative development as well. They are all closely linked.

In general, though, children do show strong emotional attachments to some toys – particularly the cuddly kind – and if dolls or soft animals are not available then they will very often use a make-shift version of something to carry around and take to bed and 'love' instead. So never deprive boys or girls of their bedtime companions. They will grow out of them in time, but they may be well into their teens before 'teddy' or a favourite rabbit is abandoned.

Toys are important too in developing children's relationships with one another, and with adults. Very small children who are taken to play with friends usually do no such thing. They cling onto their own toys and eye their companions fairly warily for the length of the visit. Playing together develops slowly, with practice and with many a set-back, as sharing and co-operating with other children becomes temporarily too difficult for them. Co-operative play does come with time and experience, though, and so it is important that some toys and games should demand the attention of more than one child from as early an age as possible. Then the lessons of sharing and the rewards of co-operating with other people will gradually become apparent.

CHOOSING BOOKS FOR CHILDREN

It is never too early for parents to give a baby a first book,

207

and most bookshops will be able to supply the indestructible kind which will stand up to being chewed or even dropped in the bath. At first small children will only focus on pictures, though they soon learn to listen to a simple story and will learn it by heart so that they can pretend to read themselves very quickly.

So, it is never too soon to start looking at books with young children, and never too early to start reading aloud with them, a pastime which can continue with great pleasure on both sides long after children have begun to read fluently themselves. In many families a story at bedtime is a tradition which is much loved and helps to bring parents and children together in a way which nothing else does.

There are good practical reasons for providing children with books and reading with them too. Long before the start of school, the child who has been read to regularly will have realized that books can be fun, that they contain stories, both comic and tragic, and are also a source of factual information. By being introduced to a wide range of books they will also have begun to extend their vocabulary beyond their own home and neighbourhood. They may never have seen a forest, or an airport, a Red Indian or a volcano, but books will have given them some idea of what to expect, and how the world works. In straightforwardly mechanical terms, they will have learned that the marks on the page themselves have a meaning, that the text goes from top to bottom and left to right (in English) and, by the time they are four or five, they may have begun to recognize a few simple words for themselves.

All the experts on learning to read emphasize how important an early introduction to books is and how vital it is to children's ability to learn well later in school to have had a happy and enthusiastic start at home. And there is increasing evidence that progress is faster during the early years of schooling if parents continue to read with their children in co-operation with the school.

SOME DO'S AND DON'T'S FOR READING ALOUD

1. Make it a regular part of a child's routine.
2. Make sure you have enough time to be able to relax with the child and not feel under any pressure to finish.
3. Choose books and stories that you both enjoy, and read slowly for understanding, allowing time to look at the pictures and, if necessary, ask and answer questions about the book.
4. Vary the material – as well as straightforward story-books, choose some collections of poems and nursery rhymes, and some factual books.
5. If you can't afford to buy a wide range of books use the local children's library.
6. Start with simple picture-books and progress to more complicated texts. Even children of ten and eleven appreciate being read to, particularly if the book is rather difficult for their level of reading ability.
7. If the book is a long one, choose an exciting place to end the episode each night, so that you both have something to look forward to when you start again.
8. As the child's own interests and preferences develop, allow these to be reflected in the reading matter: but do try to encourage children of both sexes to continue reading both fact and fiction.
9. Encourage the child to ask for an explanation if there is a word or a sentence that is not easily understood. But don't upset the flow or the enjoyment by interrogating the child about vocabulary. The meaning may be clear even though they cannot absolutely define each individual word of the text.

10. Once a child can read fluently, vary the routine by reading alternate pages. But do not force the pace. If they simply want to listen there is no harm in that.
11. Encourage children to follow up what they have been reading, either by reading themselves, or by looking for other material about whatever may have sparked their interest in a book: planes, Romans, planets or frogs in the local pond.

WHAT TO BUY, BEG OR BORROW

The children's book market is now as complex and well-stocked as that for adults, although good children's bookshops are still thin on the ground (some exceptions are listed on pages 217-19). Most of the major retailing chains which stock books, however, do usually have a children's department, and will order anything which is not in stock. And, as mentioned above, children's libraries are invaluable for families with limited funds to spend on relatively expensive books.

The early years of childhood are relatively easy to cope with, as children's individuality has not yet developed far. Most young children will be happy to have available a selection of picture-books with a simple text, a collection of bedtime stories for an adult to read aloud to them, a book of nursery rhymes and children's songs and poetry, and an ABC and a counting book.

By the age of four or five it is important to add some books which children can begin to read for themselves, and to include rather more complex fairy-tales and legends, some simple factual books and possibly a simple encyclopaedia or 'word book' through which they will extend their vocabulary from illustrations.

Later, children's need for factual information will develop and it is helpful to have access to a simple atlas, dictionary and some reference books on history, science and the other subjects which are beginning to be studied at school. At this stage, too, children's taste in stories is beginning to become more individual. Some will love adventure stories, some will prefer science-fiction, some look for humorous stories or domestic dramas. Often children will turn to a story because they have seen an adaptation of it on television, or will be interested to follow up TV characters presented in book form. Some young teenagers actually drift away from fiction altogether, and it may need some persuasion on the part of parents and teachers to get them to open a novel of any sort. But even if they insist on reading only factual books, it is still important to encourage them to keep on reading at all costs. Reading ability does not ever really stop developing.

Parents who do not have easy access to a local bookshop will find some of the guides to children's books invaluable. One example is the *Good Book Guide to Children's Books*, published by Penguin, which lists suitable books for all ages, from babies to young adults, and includes sections on poetry, cartoons, factual books, reference books and hobbies and games. With that as a source, it should be possible for any family to gain access to the very wide range of children's books now being published.

17
CONCLUSION

The education system in Great Britain – some of the changes of the 1988 Education Reform Act are being introduced in modified form in Scotland and Northern Ireland – are profound and will inevitably in the long run affect the independent as well as State sector schools. Parents and professionals seem on the whole to approve of the objectives of at least some parts of the new legislation, particularly those which can potentially raise standards. No one disputes that the general level of education of the majority of school-leavers in this country is too low and that our future depends upon raising it – quickly.

But parents in particular also need to be aware that there are quite major problems which stand in the way of the successful implementation of much that has been legislated for, not least the low morale of the teaching profession which claims that it is overworked, un-appreciated and underpaid. As a result there are serious shortages of teachers right across the country, particularly in some of the specialist areas of study like science and technology upon which the success of the National Curriculum depends. There are also shortages of books and equipment in some areas, and a high proportion of school buildings are in a desperate state of disrepair.

There are probably two things which parents can do during the 1990s to see their children safely through the rapidly evolving school system. The first is to gain as much understanding as they can of just what is going on, of which parts of the 1988 Act have general support, and which may need modification over time. I hope that this book will help with that. With such understanding they should feel able to support teachers where they will undoubtedly need support over the next few years, not least in obtaining the resources which are needed to make the best of the 1988 reforms a working reality.

The second course of action requires even more commitment. It is to participate actively themselves not just in their own child's education but in the running of the school system. The 1988 Act, and some of the preceding legislation, does put parents in a new position of partnership with the professionals and the local politicians in running State schools. But that partnership will only work if enough parents can find the time, confidence and enthusiasm to play the new role they have been offered.

What the 1988 Act and all that follows from it really demands is parents who are prepared to be active. My hope is that those parents will be found, and that the parts of the 1988 Act which have been generally welcomed as providing a real opportunity for raising standards will be turned into reality by the efforts of professionals and parents together.

18

SOURCES OF INFORMATION

NATIONAL BODIES

Commission for Racial Equality, Elliot House, 10-12 Allington Street, London SW1E 5EH. (Tel: 01-828 7022)

Curriculum Council for Wales, Castle Buildings, Womanby Street, Cardiff CF1 9SX. (Tel: 0222 34946/388150)

The Department of Education and Science, Elizabeth House, York Road, London SE1 7PH. (Tel: 01-934 9000)

Department of Education for Northern Ireland, Rathgael House, Balloo Road, Bangor, County Down BT19 2PR. (Tel: Bangor 466311)

Equal Opportunities Commission, 1 Bedford Street, WC2. (Tel: 01-379 6323)

Equal Opportunities Commission, Overseas House, Quay Street, Manchester, M3 3HN. (Tel: 01-833 9244)

National Curriculum Council, 15-17 New Street, York YO1 2RA. (Tel: York [0904] 622533)

Northern Ireland Curriculum Council, Stranmillis College, Stranmillis Road, Belfast BT9 5DY. (Tel: 0232 381414)

School Examinations and Assessment Council, Newcombe House, 45 Notting Hill Gate, London W11 3JB. (Tel: 01-229 1234)

Scottish Consultative Council on the Curriculum, 17 St. John Street, Edinburgh EH8 8DG. (Tel: 031-557 4888)

Scottish Education Department, New St, Andrews House, St James's Centre, Edinburgh EH12 5DR. (Tel: 1031-566 8400)

Welsh Education Department, Welsh Office, Cathays Park, Cardiff CF1 3NQ. (Tel: Cardiff [0222] 82511)

PARENTS' ORGANIZATIONS

Advisory Centre for Education (ACE) Ltd, 18, Victoria Park Square, London E2 3PB. (Tel: 01-980 4596)

Campaign for the Advancement of State Education, The Grove, 110 High St., Sawston, Cambs. CB2 4HJ. (Tel: 0223 833179)

Education Otherwise, 25 Common Lane, Hemingford Abbots, Cambs., PE18 9AN. (Tel: St Ives 63130)

National Association for Primary Education, Institute of Education, University of London, 20 Bedford Way, London WC1H 0AL. (Tel: 01-636 1500)

National Association for the Support of Small Schools, 91 King St., Norwich NR1 1PH. (Tel: Norwich [0603] 613088)

National Confederation of Parent-Teacher Associations, 2 Ebbsfleet Industrial Estate, Stonebridge Road, Gravesend, Kent DA11 9DZ. (Tel: [0474] 560618)

Parent-Teacher Associations of Wales, 5 St. Bridws Close, Llanyrafon, Cwmbran, Gwent NP44 8SL. (Tel: Cwmbran [0633] 34067)

UNDER FIVES

The British Association for Early Childhood Education, Studio 3:2, 140 Tabernacle Street, London EC2A 4SD. (Tel: 01-250 1768)

Pre-School Playgroups Association, 61/3 Kings Cross Road, London WC1X 9LL. (Tel: 01-833 0991)

Scottish Pre-school Play Association, 14 Elliot Place, Glasgow G3 8EP. (Tel: 041-221 4148)

SCHOOL GOVERNORS

National Association of Governors and Managers, 81 Rustlings Road, Sheffield, S11 7AB, Sheffield. (Tel: [0742] 662467)

INDEPENDENT SCHOOLS

Gabbitas-Thring Educational Trust Ltd, Broughton House, 6/8 Sackville Street, London W1X 2BR. (Tel: 01-734 0161)

Independent Schools Information Service (ISIS), 56 Buckingham Gage, London SW1E 6AG. (Tel: 01-630 8793/4)

HIGHER EDUCATION

National Union of Students, Nelson Mandela House, 461 Holloway Road, London N7 6LJ. (Tel: 01-272 8900)

Open University, Walton Hall, Milton Keynes MK7 6AA. (Tel. Milton Keynes 652026)

Polytechnics and Colleges Admissions System, PO Box 67, Cheltenham, Glos., GL50 3AP. (Tel: 0242 227788)

Universities' Central Council for Admissions, PO Box 28, Cheltenham, Glos., GL50 1HY. (Tel: Cheltenham [0242] 222444)

CAREERS

Careers and Occupational Information Centre, Moorfoot, Sheffield, S1 4PQ. (Tel: Sheffield [0742] 704563)

Careers Research and Advisory Centre (CRAC), Sheraton House, Castle Park, Cambridge, CB3 0AX.
(Tel: Cambridge [0223] 460277)

CHILDREN WITH SPECIAL NEEDS

Invalid Children's Aid Nationwide, 198 City Road, London EC1V 2PH. (Tel: 01-608 2462)

National Association for Gifted Children, 1 South Audley Street, London W1Y 5DQ. (Tel: 01-499 1188)

National Bureau for Handicapped Students (NBHS),
336 Brixton Road, London SW9 7HA. (Tel: 01-733 7977)

National Bureau for Students with Disabilities (SKILL),
336 Brixton Road, London SW9 7HA. (Tel: 01-737 7166)

National Council for Special Education, 1 Wood Street,
Stratford upon Avon CV37 6JE. (Tel: Stratford-upon-
Avon 205332)

A SELECT LIST OF CHILDREN'S BOOKSHOPS

Academy Library Services, 12 Kilbrack Lawn, Blackrock,
Cork, Ireland. (Tel: 294067)

At the Sign of the Dragon, The Bookshop (East Sheen), 131
Sheen Lane, East Sheen, London SW14 8AE.
(Tel: 01-876 3855)

The Book Boat, PO Box 347, Cutty Sark Gardens, London
SE10 9DB. (Tel: 01-853 4383)

The Book Centre, 10 High Street, Kilkenny, County
Kilkenny, Ireland. (Tel: 62117)

The Bookshop, 11 Post Street, Godmanchester,
Cambridgeshire, PE18 8BA. (Tel: 0480 55020)

Browsers, 26 Allandale Road, Stoneygate, Leicester,
Leicestershire, LE2 2DA. (Tel: 0533 701684)

Children's Book Centre Ltd., 237 Kensington High Street,
London, W8. (Tel: 01-937 7497)

Children's Bookshop, 29 Fortis Green Road, Muswell Hill,
London, N10 3RT. (Tel: 01-444 5500)

Children's Bookshop, 66 High Street, Wimbledon Village,
London, SW19 5EE. (Tel: 01-947 2038)

The Children's Bookshop (Huddersfield), 37-39 Lidget Street,
Lindley, Huddersfield, West Yorkshire, HD3 3JF. (Tel:
0484 658013)

The Children's Shop, 6A Parchment Street, Winchester,
Hampshire, SO23 8AT. (Tel: 0962 66297)

Child's Play (Hull), 78 Chanterlands Avenue, Hull, Humberside, HU5 3TS. (Tel: 0482 43580)

Duddon Books, 2 St George's Road, Millom, Cumbria, AI8 5BA. (Tel: 0657 4307)

Educational Company Ltd., 47-49 Queen Street, Belfast, County Antrim, Northern Ireland, BT1 6HP. (Tel: 0232 324687)

Foyle's Educational Ltd., Feldon House, Victoria Way, Burgess Hill, West Sussex, RH15 9NG. (Tel: 04446 2797)

Gray's Bookshop, Shopping Centre, Athlone, County Westmeath, Ireland. (Tel: 74497)

Heffers Children's Bookshop, 29-30 Trinity Street, Cambridge, Cambridgeshire, CB2 1TB. (Tel: 0223 356200)

Higham Ferrers Bookshop, 3 College Street, Higham Ferrers, Northamptonshire, NN9 8DX.
(Tel: 0933 3217222)

Jenners Princes Street Edinburgh Ltd., 48 Princes Street, Edinburgh, Lothian, Scotland, EH2 2YT. (Tel: 031-225 2442)

Kay Books, 15 High Street, Boston, Lincolnshire, PE21 85H. (Tel: 0205 64423)

The McDonald Book Company Ltd., 173 Sunbridge Road, Bradford, West Yorkshire, BD1 2HB. (Tel: 0274 724429)

John Miller, 38 Marischal Street, Peterhead, Grampian, Scotland, AB4 6HS. (Tel: 0779 72150)

Oundle School Bookshop, 13 Market Place, Oundle, Peterborough, Cambridgeshire, PE8 4BA.
(Tel: 0832 273523)

Owl Bookshop Ltd., 211 Kentish Town Road, London, NW5 2JU. (Tel: 01-485 7793)

The Pied Piper Bookshop, 108 Hutton Road, Shenfield, Essex, CM14 8NB. (Tel: 0277 219908)

The Puffin Bookshop, 1 The Market, Covent Garden, London, WC2E 8RA. (Tel: 01-379 6465)

The Rainbow Bookshop, Nutgrove Shopping Centre, Rathfarnham, Dublin, County Dublin, Ireland 14.
(Tel: 0001-932957)

Rhyme and Reason Books Ltd., 22 Malcolm Arcade, Silver Street, Leicester, Leicestershire LE1 5FT. (Tel: 0533 24591)

Simply Read, 140 Comiston Road, Edinburgh, Lothian, Scotland, EH10 5QN. (Tel: 031-447 0541)

Steps, 171 Cowbridge Road East, Canton, Cardiff, South Glamorgan, Wales. (Tel: 0222 223719)

Steps, 80 Albany Road, Roath, Cardiff, South Glamorgan, Wales. (Tel: 0222 484630)

Steps, 48 Merthyr Road, Whitchurch, Cardiff, South Glamorgan, Wales, CF4 1DJ. (Tel: 0222 625762)

Stockbridge Bookshop, 26 North West Circus Place, Edinburgh, Lothian, Scotland, EH3 6TP.
(Tel: 031-225 5355)

Stockbridge Bookshop, 43 Waverly Market, Princes Street, Edinburgh, Lothian, Scotland EH1 1BQ. (Tel: 031-557 1415)

Storyteller, 40 High Street, Billericay, Essex, CM12 9BQ. (Tel: 0277 650686)

BIBLIOGRAPHY

REFERENCE BOOKS

Education Authorities Directory, (annual), The School Government Publishing Company

Education Year Book (annual), Longman

Degree Course Guides, Careers Research and Advisory Centre

Degree Course Offers, ed. Brian Heap, Career Consultants, 1989

Directory of Further Education, Careers Research and Advisory Centre

GENERAL BOOKS

Anything School Can Do, You Can Do Better, Maire Mullarney, Arlen House, 1983

Be Your Child's Natural Teacher, Geraldine Taylor, Penguin, 1987

Children and the Law, Maggie Rae, Longman, 1986

Children's Minds, Margaret Donaldson, Fontana, 1984

Choosing a School, Felicity Taylor, Advisory Centre for Education (ACE), 1981

Closely Observed Children, Michael Armstrong, Writers' and Readers' Publishing Co-Op, 1981

The Education Reform Act: Choice and Control, ed. Denis Lawton, Hodder, 1989

Good Book Guide to Children's Books, ed. Taylor, Bing and Braithwaite, Penguin, 1984

Governors' Handbook, Foreword by Joan Sallis, ACE

How Children Learn, John Holt, Pelican, 1984

The National Curriculum, ed. Denis Lawson and Clyde Chitty, Bedford Way Series, Institute of Education, University of London, 1989

Parents' Rights in Education, Felicity Taylor, Longman, 1986

The Read-Aloud Handbook, Jim Trelease, Penguin, 1984

Schools, Parents and Governors: A New Approach to Accountability, Joan Sallis, Routledge, 1988

Special Education Handbook: New Law on Children with Special Needs, Peter Newell, ACE, 1983

Special Handbook of Research and Practice, ed. Wang, Pergamon, 1989

Summary of the 1988 Education Reform Act, Joan Sallis, ACE

Take Care, Mr Baker, The Advice on Educational Reform which the Government Collected but Concealed, ed. Julian Haviland, Fourth Estate, 1988

Teach Your Own, John Holt, Wildwood House, 1982

Young Children Learning, Barbara Tizard and Martin Hughes, Fontana Original, 1984

INDEX

223